Jillian E. Cooke

The Key to a Happy Life

St. Maximilian Kolbe's Teaching on
Contemplation and Action

IMMACULATA PRESS
531 East Merced Avenue, West Covina, CA 91790
Tel. 626.917.0040
E-mail: fkmissionaries@gmail.com

Cover design and layout by
Judith Hernandez

© 2012 Immaculata Press
531 East Merced Avenue
West Covina, California 91790
626-917-0040
fkmissionaries@gmail.com
www.kolbemission.org

Printed in the United States of America

To

the Immaculata
TOTUS TUUS

her knight
Fr. Luigi M. Faccenda, OFM Conv.
1920-2005

and his daughters
the Fr. Kolbe Missionaries of the Immaculata

"Also you!
Offer yourself to the Immaculata!
Permit Her to work through you
and you will spread much happiness upon the earth,
even in our time.
To many restless souls,
you will offer peace and serenity in God."

— *Saint Maximilian Mary Kolbe, OFM Conv.*

Table of Contents

Preface

This work was originally a thesis titled *Union with God in Action: The Relationship of Contemplation and Action in the Thought of St. Maximilian Mary Kolbe, OFM Conv.* It was submitted to the faculty of Holy Apostles College and Seminary, in Cromwell, Connecticut in partial fulfillment of a Master's Degree in Dogmatic Theology. It would have been impossible without the insight and example of Fr. Luigi Faccenda, OFM Conventual.

One will notice that Fr. Faccenda is often quoted within the text of this thesis. One who is familiar with his writings, especially *One More Gift*, will note a similar language. This, quite frankly, is unavoidable. Fr. Faccenda has lent to Kolbean studies, specifically to the study of the total consecration to the Immaculata, a vast treasure of clarified language and practical application. Through the Fr. Kolbe Missionaries of the Immaculata, this language and depth of understanding spread throughout Italy, then to Argentina, the United States, Poland, Bolivia, Luxembourg, and Brazil. With such a vast audience as this already introduced to this language, it would be futile and even detrimental to attempt to employ my own vocabulary or mode of expression.

At the same time, one will notice significant difference between this thesis and the writings of Fr. Faccenda, even from his *Symbiosis: Contemplation and Action*. There are the obvious differences in style, which is easily attributed to the difference in age, tradition, and culture. Further, in Fr. Faccenda's *Symbiosis: Contemplation and Action*, only one very small portion is dedicated explicitly to Fr. Kolbe's thought. Certainly, the entire book (small in itself) is infused with his spirit, but without already knowing the writings of Fr. Kolbe it is impossible to understand why Fr. Kolbe thinks the way that he does.

Personally, I had very little exposure to the writings of Fr. Kolbe. However, I knew the story of his life. I knew that he was a man of deep prayer, great activity, and that he was a joyful man. I reasoned that there must be a connection between the total consecration to Mary, prayer, activity, and happiness. Thus began a fourteen-month quest for a glimpse into the heart of the Kolbean spirituality.

Naturally, a heart such as Fr. Kolbe's and the question of our happiness and holiness cannot be fully explored and answered in some sixty pages. My only hope is that when you have finished this small text you have at least a more illumined vision of our awesome mission to be united to God in action. While I do not consider myself the best one to offer these insights, I have been inspired by the work of Fr. Faccenda, moved by the legacy, spirit, and brilliance of St. Maximilian Kolbe, supported and encouraged by the Fr. Kolbe Missionaries of the Immaculata, and built up by the Militia of the Immaculata. So, it is with trust in the Immaculate Conception that I repeat the words of Fr. Faccenda:

"My dear brothers and sisters, I invite you to think carefully about this spiritual writing. I am certain that, in this way, the Church will have in its heart Christians who are able to harmonize contemplation and action."

Share this joy with the world.

United in Prayer and Mission,
Jillian E. Cooke

There is little doubt that everyone in the world wants to be happy, and perhaps just as little doubt that few people are truly happy. The reality of the quest for happiness has been preached from the pulpit and is the theme often appearing in major secular publications. When people are found who are genuinely happy amidst an apparently sorrowful circumstance, they are hailed as wonders of humanity and perhaps even envied for tasting the fruit that seems so far out of reach. Further, there are those persons who profess a belief in eternal happiness, but are so caught up in the tears of this valley that they, too, forget to smile. In accepting the sorrows of this life, they have forgotten to accept also the joys. In short, many are those who believe that they will one day be happy – but not yet. It just is not the time. There is far too much sin and chaos, destruction and lethargy in this present age – sickness, poverty, and despair. Happiness will have to wait. Yet, there is evidence that we are meant to be happy even right now, and St. Maximilian Kolbe stands as a striking example – in lived testimony and written legacy – that we are meant to be happy even today.

To the untrained heart it seems foolish to tout St. Maximilian as a "happy saint." After all, he was born into oppression and died under it. Throughout his life, he certainly suffered it. It is equally as true, even testified, that he died with a slight smile on his face – alone, martyred, happy. He was a man who believed what he preached, and lived what he believed. And he preached happiness.

Though St. Maximilian Kolbe used the word happiness, it is clear that he meant far more than a mundane passing happiness found in this life. Rather, he clearly and emphatically professed a happiness that is rooted in union with God. This is the key to understanding how a person can be happy here and now – Fr. Kolbe teaches that union with God begins in this life and continues in perfection in the next. He puts no limits to that union, since it is the call of every person. It must be possible for those in the cloister as well as for those in the active life. In other words, happiness equals holiness. All men[1] are called to be holy. Therefore, all men are called to be happy. This certainly parallels Church teaching and sound philosophy.

Certainly this "union with God" that is our happiness and holiness occurs in varying degrees among the children of God. The intimacy varies as do the signs and effects of this union. Any honest look at the Church's saints of today and throughout history manifests this. However, there must be a commonality among them. This commonality is in the participants of union: the human soul and God. In what does this unity of human soul and divinity exist? Fr. Kolbe teaches that this union is primarily in the will. Through our obedience to God we are united to Him and experience authentic happiness. That the union is essentially in the will, a union of our will to the will of God, is the key to understanding why in fact union with God is possible in every form of life: consecrated, lay, clerical, contemplative, active, or any combination of the five.

Prayer is of the utmost importance in uniting one's will to the will of God. It is not determined as much by quantity, as quality. Vocal prayers, in particular the rosary and various ejaculations, are valuable in many ways. They are great means for increasing focus and strength in our lives. Meditation should never be dismissed, even when engaging in rigorous academic study, since it is fundamental to the spiritual life. Finally, contemplation is the highest form of prayer, precisely because it is union with God.

While St. Maximilian Kolbe iterated the importance of prayer: vocal, meditative, and contemplative, he did not in any way negate the active aspect of human existence. On the contrary, he taught that every action ought to be a response to the love of God poured out on the world. It not only finds its source in the external beauty of the world, but also in the inner reality of God's loving presence in the soul. The Church is missionary in nature, requiring action. This action, however, must be guided by the Holy Spirit, so that He acts in us. This presence enables man to do what is otherwise abhorrent to human nature, such as offering one's life for a friend.

When a soul is able to unite to the Trinity, particularly through total consecration to Mary, the Immaculata, all actions take on a divine element because they are done according to His will. Obedience is the guide for all action; trust in God's mercy is the remedy for failure to obey.

St. Maximilian Kolbe thus distinguishes contemplation from action, and yet teaches that there is a clear symbiosis between the two. Through the union of the wills our daily life becomes a field of conversion and contemplation. In contemplation our wills discover their delight. Ultimately the prayer of contemplation gives way to a mystical state, in which the Spirit (through the Immaculata) governs one's whole life.

Genuine happiness comes with holiness. St. Maximilian Kolbe's equating of happiness and holiness is not a new concept. The argument springs from the Aristotelian principle that all things in nature have an end to which they tend, and in which they find their actualization. The basic argument is as follows: natural desires are meant to be fulfilled. Happiness is a natural desire. Therefore, happiness can be attained. Following is a brief elaboration of this basic syllogism.

Natural desires are meant to be fulfilled. "In nature we see that all natural tendencies reach their actualization: the eye desires to see and it can, the ear to hear and it can, the body to nourish itself and it can."[2] There is an impulse to deny such a possibility of black and white fulfillment in happiness, and yet Fr. Kolbe poses the rhetorical question: "How could the soul's most ardent and important desire remain unfulfilled...?" Coupled with the intensity of this desire, is its universality. The desire for happiness exists in all men, as pointed out by Fr. Kolbe in this brief reflection:

Where are you going in the course of your life? You always do, think, or say something – each day, each hour. To what end? The truth is that you aspire for something more or less distant; and you tend towards it because you hope that it will bring you a crumb of happiness. This aspiration for happiness is natural. No man exists in the world who does not desire happiness. Only to find happiness men amass money, search for glory and pleasure...[3]

Fr. Kolbe holds simply that "there does not exist a man in the world who does not go in search of happiness, rather, in every one of our actions happiness presents itself to us, in one form or another, as the goal towards which we naturally tend."[4] While it is true that we search for even a "crumb" of happiness in this life, it is equally true that "no man exists under the sun that does not long for happiness, the greatest possible happiness, happiness without limit."[5] However, such happiness cannot be found in this life, on this finite earth amid finite creatures. Rather, such happiness "can only be God: infinite, eternal, heaven."[6]

If our desire for an unlimited happiness were unable to be fulfilled, it would be absolutely useless. It would be thus completely contrary to nature, which always tends towards actualization in a specific end. Because the desire for happiness exists, and is unable to be satisfied by any created thing, it must have an end, and this end must be God.

It is also possible to work backwards in this argument, positing that God is all good, as decreed by faith. The existence of our desire for happiness without an end is not only contrary to human nature, but even to the divine nature:

> In such a [hypothetical] case, this desire would be useless. ...a God that creates in nature this certain inexhaustible craving for happiness with the explicit intention that it has no limit, but does not offer the fulfillment of this ardent desire, would not act with reason nor with goodness, in a word – it would not be God. Such happiness, therefore, must exist.[7]

Regardless of whether one works from the fundamentals of human nature or from faith in an all good God, it must be concluded that a limitless happiness, towards which all men tend by nature and is possible for all men, does exist. Since it takes the infinite to satiate a limitless desire, this happiness is in God. At the same time it is impossible to have any true happiness outside of God. He is the source of happiness and whoever goes near to God participates in His[8] happiness, and already in this life foretastes [eternal] happiness."

All men tend naturally toward God. Therefore, our happiness depends on our holiness, and will thus be found in otherwise unexpected places and circumstances. Most remarkably, happiness can be found amidst even intense suffering because in suffering we are united to Christ: "To be crucified for love of the Crucified is the only happiness on earth!" "Love crosses. Cross, Cross, Cross = the source of true Happiness."[10] The eyes of faith tell us that crosses carried out of love draw us near to God, even while still in this world. Yet, the eyes of this world are definitely scandalized, or at least utterly perplexed. Suffering and union with God will be discussed in greater detail later in this thesis. For now, we conclude that happiness and holiness go hand in hand, and thus all the conclusions that have been made about happiness can and must be said about holiness. Namely, all men desire to be holy as the fulfillment of their nature, and therefore it is both universal and possible.

Getting back to the union of wills, recall that Fr. Kolbe believes it is essential to holiness and happiness, that all men are created for holiness, and that this holiness has its source in God. Next, it is necessary to determine man's relationship to this source, as the source and subject may be more or less distant from each other. The Colorado River, meandering through Arizona, has its source in the mountains of Colorado, while the source of a burn is direct contact with something very hot. It is perhaps instinctive to consider our relationship with God, as source of our holiness and happiness, more akin to the waters of the Colorado than to a burn. After all, God is infinite and we are finite, the relationship definitive, but the gap insurmountable. However, Fr. Kolbe very clearly states that our relationship with God is an intimate, intense union. This union is in the will.

Fr. Kolbe was so convinced of this reality that in his writings one can scarcely find "union with God" without the words "will of God" in close proximity. He states definitively that the grade of perfection depends on the union of our will with the will of God.[11] This union of the wills is achieved through the virtue of obedience, as the "easiest, shortest, and most certain way to holiness; ... indeed, supernatural obedience is the essence of holiness, that of perfect love."[12] The nature of obedience and its limits will be treated later in this thesis.

Uniting our will to God's will is the essence of holiness, as Fr. Kolbe stated, because it is actually the essence of love. If one wishes to be a saint, even a great saint, he needs only to will it. Such a claim requires explanation, and Fr. Kolbe gives substantial evidence – both passive and active – as he explains that love IS NOT in the sentiments or in bare action. Love IS conformity to Christ. In each case it is manifest that love must be in the will. Of this, Fr. Kolbe writes,

> Love with all your being, with all your will, and with all your sentiment. If your senses are dry, and you are not able to sustain sentiments of love, don't worry. These do not belong to the essence of love. If the will only desires to accomplish (the Immaculata's) will, be assured that you really love Her, Jesus, and the Father. Do not forget that sanctity does not consist in extraordinary actions, but in doing well your duties toward God, yourself, and others.[13]

In order to fully understand this critical text, it is important to clarify Fr. Kolbe's understanding of the role of the Immaculata in accomplishing God's will. An entire thesis could be written on this point alone. However, for the current purpose his teachings will be presented within the context of his whole thought.

Fr. Kolbe taught that to do the will of the Immaculata is to do the will of God. In fact "it is right that the accomplishment of the Will of the Immaculata 'in the littlest particulars and in the most exact manner' constitutes the highest level of sanctity, because, in effect, Her Will is the same Will of Jesus, the Will of God."[14] In order to understand this properly according to Kolbean teaching, it is essential to insist that "the Immaculata is only a work of God and, as every work, incomprehensibly inferior to Her Creator." She depends on Him completely and for everything. But, at the same time, She is the most perfect work of His creation, "the final limit between God and creation. She is a faithful image of the perfection and holiness of God."[15]

It is this perfection that makes it possible to state that "Her will is the same as God's will." Fr. Kolbe's reasoning is once again a simple syllogism. The grade of perfection depends on the union of our will with the will of God. The Immaculata is the most perfect creation, even more perfect than the angels. Therefore, it stands to reason that "Her will is united in the closest possible way with the will of God. She lives and works uniquely in God and through God. Therefore, doing the will of the Immaculata is the same as doing the will of God."[16]

Some consider this Kolbean language too strong, bordering if not completely falling into heresy by setting the Immaculata on the same level of holiness and perfection as God. In his time this objection was voiced even within his friary, giving Fr. Kolbe ample opportunity to clarify statements regarding the relationship between the will of the Immaculata and the will of God. For instance, regarding the statement, "we want only to do the will of the Immaculata," Fr. Kolbe states that "with such an affirmation we are not diminishing [*affatto*] the glory of God, but instead we increase it greatly. In this way we recognize and venerate God's omnipotence, which has given existence to a creature so sublime and perfect."[17] Therefore, without fear

14

or doubt, we state that the will of the Immaculata is the will of God, likewise to do the will of the Immaculata is to do the will of God, and similarly our perfection lies in accomplishing Her will as it does in accomplishing the will of God.

Secondly, love is conformity to Christ. Imitation of Christ is the means of this conformity. One imitates Christ primarily through a life of obedience. This much has been established, but to what does this imitation lead? Imitation of Christ leads to a spousal union with Christ, that is, an intimate union that is due both to an acquired likeness through holy obedience and divine action in the soul. In other words, the union of our will with God's will actually unites us to the person of Christ, through submission to the Father and by the power of the Spirit active in our souls. Almost suddenly, our small acts of love for God become instruments for spousal union with our love. In this thesis the relationship of our action and union with God, as taught by St. Maximilian, will be elaborated and clarified specifically as the symbiosis of contemplation and action.

Before we begin, the definitions of *contemplation* and *action* must be established. *Action*, easily enough, is anything one does. This is a definition that needs no justification. *Contemplation* is not as immediate. Since Fr. Kolbe does not define *contemplation*, it is impossible to quote him exactly. However, given all the substantial evidence up to this point regarding his understanding of man's possible intimacy with God, it is possible to conclude that *contemplation* in Kolbean thought is simply the union of the soul with God. This definition is confirmed by various writers of Kolbean spirituality, most notably by Fr. Luigi Faccenda, OFM Conv.[18] and Fr. Jean-Francois de Louvencourt, OCSO, particularly in his treatise, *St. Maximilian Kolbe: Friend and Doctor of Prayer*.[19]

Fr. Kolbe does not directly address the relationship between contemplation and action, however, his writings often centered on one or more of the following: prayer, union with God through the will, and proper Christian action. In fact, it is worth noting the consistency of his thought, even as it developed over time. Whether writing in personal notes, letters, articles for publication, or preparing to write a book, the conviction of the possibility and necessity of a real symbiosis between contemplation and action is evident. Likewise, from the time he was a novice in the seminary until his final notes only the night before his final arrest, his writings express his determination to live this symbiosis in his own life. Therefore, it is more than an intellectual theory. It is intimately connected to our humanity as Fr. Kolbe understood it.

This thesis will be fully developed in four steps. First, I will explain Fr. Kolbe's fundamental teaching that happiness and holiness have their source in supernatural obedience, which is the union of the individual human will with the divine will. This is the means to union with God. Secondly, the primacy of the interior life in the pursuit of happiness and holiness will be elaborated. Thirdly, the means and possibility of the sanctification of action will be defined. Lastly, the relationship between contemplation (union with God) and action will be specifically defined as symbiotic.

Before moving to the body of the thesis, it is important to give due attention to one particular text outside of the writings of Fr. Kolbe. *Symbiosis: Contemplation and Action*, written by Fr. Luigi Faccenda, greatly influenced this thesis. At the same time, this influence is largely with regards to the conclusion itself, rather than the actual content of the thesis. It is a relatively short work, with only a small portion dedicated specifically to Fr. Kolbe's thought. According to academic norms, Fr. Faccenda is rightly cited whenever this or any of his writings are directly quoted or his original thoughts expressed.

Notes

1   Within this work the reference to "man" signifies humanity or "mankind," that is, man and woman. The use of this term alone is for the sake of simplicity and consistency with Kolbean usage.

2   Maximilian Kolbe, Unpublished, Mugenzai no Sono, Japan, 1934-1935, in *Scritti di Massimiliano Kolbe* [Writings of Maximilian Kolbe] (Rome: Editrice Nazionale M.I., 1997), sec. 1270.

3   Ibid.

4   Kolbe, "La verità," *Rycerz Niepokalanej* [Knight of the Immaculata], December 1940-January 1941, 6-8. in *Scritti* sec. 1246.

5   Kolbe, "Non credo...," *Rycerz Niepokalanej*, August 1933, 229. in *Scritti* sec. 1169.

6   Kolbe, "Il paradiso," *Rycerz Niepokalanej*, February 1926, 36-38. in *Scritti* sec. 1116.

7   Ibid.

8   Faithful to Kolbe, pronouns referring to the Holy Trinity or the Blessed Mother will be capitalized.

9   Kolbe, "La Regina della Polonia," *Rycerz Niepokalanej*, May 1925, 97-102. in *Scritti* sec. 1093.

10   Kolbe, Spiritual Exercises, Rome 1917, in *Scritti* sec. 968.

11   Kolbe to fr. Matteo Spolitakiewicz, Nagasaki, Japan, in *Scritti* sec. 643.

12   Kolbe to Bernardo Hatada, Kobe, Japan, May 30, 1932, in *Scritti* sec. 428.

13   Kolbe, for an unpublished book, August 5-20, 1940, in *Scritti* sec. 1334.

14   Kolbe to the brothers in the Editorial Department, Zakopane, Poland, October 14, 1937, in *Scritti* sec. 748.

15   Kolbe, "Volontà di Dio e Volontà dell'Immacolata," *Informator Rycerstwa Niepokalanej* [Information of the Knights of the Immaculata], September 1938, 34. in *Scritti* sec. 1232.

16   Ibid.

17   Ibid.

18   Luigi Faccenda, *One More Gift* (West Covina, CA: Immaculata Press, 1990); "Father Kolbe, the Immaculata, and the Most Holy Trinity" (West Covina, CA: Fr. Kolbe Missionaries of the Immaculata, 1995) Conference given to the St. Bonaventure Pontifical Theological Faculty; *Symbiosis: Contemplation and Action* (West Covina, CA: Immaculata Press, 1991).

19   Jean-Francois de Louvencourt, *St. Maximilian Kolbe: Friend and Doctor of Prayer*, CD ROM, (Chicago, IL: Marytown Press).

Man's quest for happiness begins with the age-old questions: Who am I? Where am I going? In asking, man is really seeking his own fulfillment and the reason for his existence. This existence finds meaning ultimately in God. The reason for this is simple: every single person is created in the image and likeness of God. We come from God as sharing in His goodness and wisdom in our will and intellect, and we return to Him as the perfection that we seek. When man reaches toward the infinite God, and allows the infinite God to reach down to him, he is finally and truly happy. Jesus Christ bridged the gap between heaven and earth, assuring that we would not reach in vain because the good God stooped so low as to meet us here on earth. Union with God, our happiness, is possible.

Fr. Kolbe teaches that it is possible specifically through supernatural obedience, understood not as an end in itself, but as a means to union with God. Obedience is often interpreted as the suppression of our freedom, but the opposite is actually true. "The more one does what is good, the freer one becomes. There is no true freedom except in service of what is good and just."[20] Therefore, obedience is actually the key to a truly free, human life. It functions as a means to union with God, which also requires the sanctification of our actions. This ultimately manifests the relationship between contemplation and action. Therefore, beginning from the foundation, in this thesis we will look first to obedience.

As has been stated, it often carries with it a negative connotation. It also might be questioned whether obedience, in this case preached by an ordained Franciscan Friar, is limited to the consecrated life. Therefore, we must first define the nature of obedience in Kolbean thought, and whether it applies universally to man.

St. Maximilian makes a distinction between natural obedience and supernatural obedience. *Natural obedience* is nothing more than doing what one is commanded, while *supernatural obedience* is the union of our will with the divine will. This is the essence of holiness and the perfection of love. It is the latter that concerns Fr. Kolbe in his pursuit of holiness. It directed his entire life as well as his formation of others, as evidenced in much of his writing. In one magazine article, Fr. Kolbe writes to his readers: "Every one of us must be concerned only in harmonizing, conforming, merging, so to speak, our own will completely with the Immaculata's Will, just as Her Will is completely united to the Will of God, Her Heart with the Heart of Her Son Jesus."[21] He summarized his whole doctrine on holiness and obedience with the formula w=W=holiness. The lower-case 'w' represents our will and the capital 'W' the divine will.[22] Everything else is secondary, whether consolations or trials. For the remainder of the thesis, when obedience is used, it refers to this supernatural obedience.

The essence of obedience is the union of the personal will with the will of God. However, Fr. Kolbe did not leave obedience as an intangible "do good" element. Rather, in the course of his writings he supplies insight into the distinctive marks of this obedience. While he often refers to obedience in a religious community, it is clear that obedience is not limited to the members of the religious life because its fundamental nature consists in trust and the sacrifice of the will and intellect to God. Everyone can trust God, and everyone has a will and intellect to sacrifice to Him. The first enables the second; which enables union with God. This is the end of obedience. Each of these will be explained with greater clarity, flowing naturally into the presentation of contemplation.

In reality, it can be said that obedience and trust are two aspects of the same interior attitude, because obedience is the expression and the consequence of trust. Fr. Kolbe's trust was as much a matter of recognizing his personal inability as it was recognizing the immense goodness and power of God. Over and over again his writings confirm that we must not have any fear, because victory will be ours. How? By not trusting even the littlest amount in ourselves, but instead offering all of ourselves, especially all our temptations and difficulties, to the Immaculata. "Whoever turns to Her with trust throughout life, *certainly will be saved.*"[23]

It is essential to note, however, that his trust in victory was not in the temporal order, but in ultimate victory over death. Trust and obedience come together in this life. Fr. Kolbe's writings instruct us to place our trust in God, Who has ordered all things for that final victory. Such trust empowers a person to be obedient in the present moment, no matter how difficult. "We trust, therefore, in the Divine Providence, in the Will of the Immaculata, and we remain certain that God permits every good thing in view of a greater good."[24] Obedience is the means for partaking in this victory, of being happy always and everywhere. Obedience is trust in God's loving action in the world and accepting the circumstances of daily life as ordered by God for a greater good.

Now, this trust is not limited to the religious life. Clearly, Fr. Kolbe had a great love for religious obedience; this is certain and cannot be underestimated. However, his loving submission to his superiors was his submission to God's representatives. Within secular life there are ample examples of authority figures who are God's representatives through divine ordination, such as within the Magisterium, in the natural order, such as the family, and even in the temporal order, such as an employer.

Lest supernatural obedience be confused with an irresponsible blind obedience to every kind of authority, it must be clarified that one is never bound to commit sin. On the contrary he is obligated not to offend God in even the slightest manner. Further, true obedience – as noted above – increases freedom because it is the *right use* of our reason. Thus, difficult circumstances are not an excuse to sin. Spouses cannot oblige another to live or tell a lie, bosses must treat employees with dignity, etc. We must continue to use our God given intellect and will for constant discernment of the divine will.

Examples in the life of Fr. Kolbe indicate that with all his respect for authority and order, as well as a wariness to exert his own will, he never ceased to seek the will of God in an active manner. He presented his thoughts and dreams, even multiple times if at first refused. As superior he insisted on equality and transparency in dealings, and sought the input of all his friars. For this reason, I do not interpret Fr. Kolbe's concept of religious obedience to mean that directives contrary to prudence, even if they are not sinful, need to be blindly obeyed as in situations where the head of the order or the spiritual directors are demanding confidentiality where this could have very bad consequences.

Neither is obedience limited to direct obedience to a command. We are obliged to present "divine inspiration" to a responsible person for authorization, and if thereby judged as coming from God we are called to follow it. Fr. Kolbe cites the dramatic events of the apparitions of Our Lady to St. Catherine Laboure, but such inspirations include the gentle movements of the soul in everyday life. Fr. Kolbe applied this to the apostolate, insisting that every means of evangelization be according to obedience. How often he could have charged ahead zealously with great ideas and passion! Yet he cautioned and exemplified that zeal must be accompanied by prudence, including submission to another through obedience. Whether God's will is manifest to us through authority, inspiration, or circumstance, obedience unites the personal will to the divine will through trusting acceptance. This acceptance is marked by promptness, serenity, charity, generosity, and peace.

The second element of obedience, made possible only by the trust elaborated above, is sacrifice. In obedience we sacrifice, for the love of God, intellect and will. It is this sacrifice that makes obedience difficult, but also what makes it the open door to happiness – union with God in contemplation. One may be inclined to doubt this claim, either from sheer disbelief or perhaps denial, but a brief description of the human intellect and will demonstrates aptly the greatness of the sacrifice.

The intellect and will distinguish man from all other bodily creatures. It is specifically in these faculties that "the human person participates in the light and power of the divine Spirit. By his reason [intellect], he is capable of understanding the order of things established by the Creator. By free will, he is capable of directing himself toward his true good."[25] Thus, created in the image of God, the right use of will and intellect leads us to conformity to Christ through union. Such right ordering of the will and intellect directs our actions, therefore, in order to attain a true habit of supernatural obedience one must begin by fostering the interior life.

Notes

20 *Catechism of the Catholic Church*, 2nd ed., pt. III, sec. 1, ch. 1, n. 1733.

21 Kolbe, "La nostra guerra," *Rycerz Niepokalanej*, May 1932, 133-134. in *Scritti* sec. 1160.

22 Kolbe, quoted by Luigi Faccenda, *Symbiosis: Contemplation and Action* (West Covina, CA: Immaculata Press, 1991), 56.

23 Kolbe, "Il segreto della forza e della potenza," *Rycerz Niepokalanej*, September 1925, 225-227. in *Scritti* sec. 1100.

24 Kolbe to fr. Rocco Frejlich, Niepokalanów, Poland, January 9, 1941, in *Scritti* sec. 935.

25 *Catechism*, pt. III, sec. 1, ch. 1, n. 1704.

The Primacy of the Interior Life

The *interior life* is used in comparison to the *external life* and is understood as that part of man that is highest in him, the will and intellect, the faculties of the soul, and the movements therein. The external life refers to all that is seen and corporal. The two are distinct, but intimately related, as having the body and soul as their proper subjects. Fr. Kolbe's teaching on obedience indicates that the external life is perfected through subjection to the interior life. This relationship will be further investigated in the final section of this thesis. Now we turn specifically to the interior life.

Up to this point, a foundation has been laid that establishes man as coming from God, created in His image and likeness, and going toward God as his ultimate happiness. This happiness has been defined as holiness with its source in God. Happiness, therefore, is the union of the soul with God. This union results from a union of the will of man with the will of God in supernatural obedience. Essentially, when we habitually choose the good as presented to us by the intellect, our union with God increases. If our ultimate happiness is union with God in the perfection of this loving and knowing, it can be concluded that the interior life is essential and of primary importance to the pursuit of a happy, truly human life. Fr. Kolbe was blunt in affirming this truth:

> Our contemporaries, excessively pressed by material problems, forget prayer. From the morning to the evening they are obsessed only by a lust for gain, whether on the sea or on land, in factories or shops.

> Prayer is the expression of a beautiful soul. The human body had its origin in dust, and after death it will transform into dust. ... Only in the moment of prayer man elevates his heart toward paradise and enters into conversation with the Creator of the universe, with the first Cause of everything, with God.[26]

In prayer, we rise above the mundane things of this earth and begin to foster an authentic relationship with our God. It is only in prayer that we are able to "comprehend" the spirit of prayer, and only in prayer that we are made aware of "the happiness it offers the soul" and the "energy [it] communicates in daily life."[27] Prayer is absolutely necessary for our happiness and holiness because it is absolutely necessary for illumining the intellect and strengthening the will.

That prayer illumines the intellect is evident in Fr. Kolbe's basic definition of prayer: "Prayer is the elevation of the mind to God."[28] It is true that this definition was written as early as 1915, while he was still in the seminary. However, he often returns to this definition as it comes from the *Rule of St. Francis*, which he cites explicitly in a letter to his friars in 1939:

> I hope that all the brothers – everyone without any exception – will help us during the Chapter, not only with exterior prayer, but also with that *internal* prayer. Father St. Francis speaks of it in the *Rule* when he writes, "That the friars do not extinguish the *spirit* of prayer." The spirit of prayer consists in always elevating one's thought [*il pensiero*] to God.[29]

He goes on further to define the elevation of the mind as right intention:

> One's thought [il pensiero], namely one's *intention*, must be to act, work, rest, suffer, and even pray publicly *only* because this is the *Will of the Immaculata*, to *please* Her, and through Her, the *Most Sacred Heart of Jesus*. ... Let us pray that the Immaculata purifies and elevates our intentions always more.[30]

Therefore, a few fundamental points about prayer can be made. Prayer is the raising of the mind to God with the desire to please Him. It is this characteristic that separates prayer from any of the listed actions – activity, work, rest, suffering, and public prayer. None of these are truly prayer unless the mind is turned to God, and the will desires him as good. It must not be interpreted that Fr. Kolbe holds that all one needs to do is "do things for God" in order to live a life of prayer. This would be paramount to natural obedience, like a skeleton without flesh or a body without a soul.

The spirit of prayer gives our otherwise merely natural activities a supernatural quality. However, it does not encompass the totality of prayer any more than doing things in the "spirit of America" encompasses the United States. Rather, there is a clear gradation of prayer leading up to contemplation, which is prayer par excellence. We will see that only in this prayer is the mind truly elevated to God. In summary, we turn to an excerpt from an article written by Fr. Kolbe for the *Rycerz Niepokalanej*:

> Only Jesus, coming into the world, indicated to humanity the road to true sanctity through example and word. The substance of which is to love God unto heroism. The distinctive sign is the accomplishment of the Divine Will, contained above all in the commandments of God and the Church, and in the duties of one's state (in life). The means is the constant vigilance over oneself, with the end of knowing ones defects and uproot them, to graft virtues, to cultivate them, to develop them to the highest degree. Then, there is prayer, with which the soul procures supernatural divine graces, which are indispensable to spiritual progress. In all the saints prayer occupies a place of prime importance.[31]

The article then states that the most important degrees of prayer are vocal, meditative, and contemplative. Presently, each degree will be explained in the context of Kolbean thought, with special attention paid to contemplation as the highest, most perfect form of prayer. It is the prayer that most perfectly unites us to God and infuses us most perfectly with the spirit of prayer.

Perhaps one may consider it a waste to develop vocal and meditative prayer, since our actual goal is to have an understanding of contemplation. However, while we are interested in contemplation for its own sake, it is the pinnacle of a gradation of prayer. In order to understand this pinnacle, we must begin at the foundation. No grand building, no building at all, can stand without a solid foundation.

The breadth of prayer is wide, to be sure, so wide that one form often blends with other forms of prayer. For example, one vocally prays the rosary, while meditating on the mysteries, and in the case of some this leads to a real contemplation. It must not be assumed that these three gradations of prayer can be categorized into black and white boxes. Rather, they blend together like a color scale; it is often unclear where one begins and the other ends. In order to reach the purity of contemplative prayer, one must begin in the "black," deliberate vocal prayer.

Prayer is absolutely necessary. Fr. Kolbe encourages his brothers:

> In effect, prayer is a hidden, yet most efficacious, means to restore peace in souls and to give them happiness because it serves to draw souls to the love of God. Prayer renews the world. Prayer is the indispensable condition for the regeneration and life of every soul. ... Let us also pray, and pray well, and pray much, whether with the lips or with the mind [*il pensiero*].[32]

This admonition draws out an important connection between vocal prayer (whether with the lips or with the mind) and our ultimate end of happiness. It also points out the consequential experience of peace and joy found in a soul that is drawn close to God. We cannot have one without the other.

There is no shortage in Kolbean teaching regarding the many vocal prayers and their efficacy in the development of the interior life. The miraculous medal and the holy rosary are two devotionals highly recommended by Fr. Kolbe. Other Kolbean favorites are various ejaculations, the prayer of the miraculous medal, the doxology, the names of Jesus and Mary, the Franciscan crown, and the list goes on. Superior to all other forms of prayer is the liturgical worship of God, first in the Holy Mass, in Adoration, and in the Divine Office. One must be reminded, especially with regard to these liturgical prayers, that true vocal prayer is not an end in itself. It moves the individual to a more perfect interior life.

This leads to the next degree of prayer: meditation. The link between the vocal prayer and meditation is clarified in one of Fr. Kolbe's notes from his days in the seminary: "Before meditation, make a humble prayer."[33] Clearly, this humble prayer is a simple vocal prayer, which he classically divided into prayers of intercession, adoration, and contrition.[34] Vocal prayer literally precedes meditation, and the two are very often blended as stated above. However, prayer takes on a properly meditative nature when it is purely intellectual, as a properly interior prayer. This intellectual activity must be imbued with the spirit of prayer, understood as discussed above, in order to be prayer at all. Otherwise it remains an activity of the intellect only, which is inferior to true meditation, as he expressed while he was still very young: "Devotion, prayer (meditation, according to the rule) is the principal duty, not study. *Pietas et scienza. Ora et labora*; non: *labora et ora.* [Piety and science. Pray and work; not: work and pray.]"[35]

He took this duty seriously, reminding himself never to neglect meditation. In this, he was motivated by the saints: "When they could not meditate in the day, the saints meditated during the night, and so they converted so many persons."[36] Three points ought to be made regarding Fr. Kolbe's meditation, which taken together serve as the bridge between vocal prayer and contemplation. 1. Meditation must be prepared. Human effort is definitely required. 2. Meditation, though cognitive, is also a prayer of discourse with the Lord. 3. Meditation is not an end in itself. Especially when meditating on the passion of Christ it opens one to the imitation of Christ.[37] "*Meditation on the Passion of Jesus is the most efficacious means to arouse in oneself sorrow for sins and to flare up love for Jesus.*"[38]

Meditating on the Passion of Jesus, the intellect comes to know Christ more. Two things result: the rightful deprecation of self, which is an authentic humility (sorrow for sins) that is required for any real obedience, and rightful awareness of God as the Good, which in turn enables the will to love that good. The end result is that the intellect and the will are more disposed to the grace of God. There is a deeper freedom and a greater humility, resulting in authentic charity. Since the will's proper act is to love, then we reiterate that union with God is in charity. Therefore, acts of supernatural obedience are sure acts of love that unite us to God as our will is united to His will. We also have discussed the role of the intellect as knowing God and presenting this Truth to the will as the good it seeks. The will is thus able to choose (love) Him.

Fr. Kolbe did not explicitly define contemplation, yet it is clear from his writings that he gave it primacy of place and loved it dearly. He listed it in the gradation of prayer as the highest form. His favorite saints were passionate contemplatives: St. Gemma Galgani, St. Francis of Assisi, and St. Therese of the Child Jesus. He wrote here and there of the great work done in the cloisters, even of their great missionary work (speaking very often specifically of St. Therese), and of the need for prayers from the contemplatives. And yet, while Fr. Kolbe refers to those in the contemplative life as persons living lives behind the walls of a cloister, it would contradict his teachings on obedience and union with God to suggest that he thought contemplation was restricted only to those living such a life.

One can imagine that Fr. Kolbe would have become a contemplative if he had considered it the only path to union with God. While the "contemplative life" fosters a life of contemplation, the cloistered contemplatives are not the sole heirs of this gift. Considering the scope of the present thesis, the foundation of Fr. Kolbe's emphasis on love through obedience as union with God, and his Franciscan heritage, we share Fr. Louvencourt's conclusion. He contends that contemplation in Kolbean thought can be defined according to

St. Bonaventure (and in agreement with St. John of the Cross) as "an act of knowledge and an act of the will. The two are inseparable, but the entire essence of contemplation consists in an 'extremely ardent passion' of love. ... Contemplation is not an exceptional gift, but the normal end of a preceding path."[39]

It is true that "in this stage of prayer God sometimes drags the soul very near to Himself. In such a case the soul is bathed in an otherworldly light and enflamed by love. The soul enters ecstasy that has nothing in common with natural enchantments. However, this is dispensable and unnecessary for sanctity."[40] Rather, "we only have to desire [will] it."[41] "When a soul does what it can, grace easily elevates it and this is the work of God."[42] Contemplation cannot be produced through human effort; one can only dispose himself through prayer and lively desire.

It is for this reason that Fr. Kolbe frequently insisted that people pray every day and at every instant. Prayer accomplishes the three things that make union with God possible. It illumines the intellect to know the truth, which is presented to the will. Prayer makes it possible for the will to consistently choose this as good, which is to say that prayer makes it possible to love. Prayer strengthens the will to choose the good over the false and/or lesser goods of the senses and thereby serve God. Finally, it purifies one's intentions, so that they are ordered to a true spirit of prayer.[43] Illumined, strengthened, and purified in prayer, willing to be united to God through the excellent grace of contemplation, in the end we depend entirely on God to bestow it.

We must not fall into the trap of jumping from stage to stage as though they were right-angled steps, clearly marked and easily scaled. The analogy of a scale of color still holds true, perhaps especially within contemplation itself. Here we speak of God's direct action on the soul, an action that is at once mysterious and evident. As Fr. Kolbe stated, God "drags" a soul to himself and only He knows what exterior manifestations will result. Only God knows to what degree the soul is immersed in

His loving Trinity and vice versa. The human person must respond to this love in the manner and to the degree that he is able.

All human beings are active. They must act. Eating, sleeping, working, and speaking are all activities. Therefore, even the souls in the cloister cannot escape their bodies, nor should they. It follows that this response to God's love must involve activity. The interior life therefore maintains primacy, but the exterior life – the life of activity – is of great value in attaining holiness and happiness. Ultimately we will clearly define the relationship between action and contemplation, but first let us investigate action as understood by Fr. Kolbe in the context of the pursuit of our happiness.

Notes

26   Kolbe, "La preghiera," *Mugenzai no Seibo no Kishi*, June 1936, 2ff. in *Scritti* sec. 1208.

27   Ibid.

28   Kolbe, Spiritual Exercises, Rome 1915, in *Scritti* sec. 965.

29   Kolbe to Niepokalanów, Krakow, Poland, August 22, 1939, in *Scritti* sec. 878.

30   Ibid.

31   Kolbe, "La santità," *Rycerz Niepokalanej*, March 1922, 45-47. in *Scritti* sec. 1001.

32   Kolbe to Mugenzai no Sono, Niepokalanów, September 10, 1940, in *Scritti* sec. 903.

33   Kolbe, Spiritual Exercises, Rome 1915.

34   Ibid.

35   Ibid.

36   Ibid.

37   See Jean-Francois de Louvencourt, *St. Maximilian Kolbe: Friend and Doctor of Prayer*, CD ROM, (Chicago, IL: Marytown Press) pt. 4.

38   Kolbe, Spiritual Exercises, Rome 1915.

39   Louvencourt, pt. 1.

40   Kolbe, "La santità."

41   Ibid.

42   Louvencourt, pt. 1.

43   Kolbe to Niepokalanów, Krakow, August 22, 1939, in *Scritti* sec. 878. See also Kolbe, Spiritual Exercises, Rome 1915.

The first point to establish when approaching the topic of action as it relates to our happiness and holiness is the fact that, according to Kolbe, this world is intrinsically good. Fr. Kolbe was convinced of this, and held tenaciously to this belief throughout his life. He was not immune to the familiar pains of human frustration, anxiety, and despair.[44] Yet, he looked to God as Creator in order to find goodness in all of creation. He comes to this conclusion simply through the relation of cause and effect: "An effect is similar to its cause. [God is the cause of creation.] Consequently, every creature bears within itself the likeness of God ..."[45]

In a moment of typical Kolbean zeal while riding on a train, Fr. Kolbe challenged a fellow passenger to recognize an intelligent creator based on the order in the universe. Then, using arguments based on Thomistic-Aristotelian causality, he proceeded to demonstrate that all effects exist in some more perfect way in a cause:

> Let's take a painter. He gives nothing of himself to the painting, neither color nor canvas; all this he takes from outside himself. Still, he gives something that is the form that he has within himself. First, he had to imagine this painting within himself, before taking the paintbrush in hand; in the second place he painted based on a model that was formed in the mind and imagination. God, however, took nothing from outside Himself; being the first cause He drew His own work from nothing, He gave everything to this work, so that every perfection present in creatures must be also in Him, but in a way, as I stated before, infinitely perfect, since in Him there can be no limitations.[46]

God, then, is the "painter" of creation, who gives everything to His masterpiece. Since God is all simple, it may be said in a classic idiomatic expression turned reality: He pours Himself into His work. All creation comes from Him, and therefore in varying degrees bears a likeness to Him. Man is the creature actually created in His image (imago Dei) and therefore he is a particularly true reflection of God in the created universe. All creation is understood, and man specifically, with reference to this divine life.

Fr. Kolbe wrote: "God is Love (1 Jn 4:16). In the fullness of this life the Father generates the Son, while the Spirit proceeds from the Father and the Son."[47] At another moment, he wrote: "God knows Himself, loves (Himself), and so the Father generates the Son and the Holy Spirit proceeds from the Father and the Son."[48] But, we know that this divine life, this divine love, does not remain exclusive. In the great Franciscan thesis, of which St. Maximilian was a proponent, God willed "co-lovers"[49] – outside of Himself – to share in His love. Christ is that "co-lover" par excellence for which all creation came to be in existence. Man created in Christ's image, participates in that same love. Because God is all simple and He is love, all creation shares in this one act of eternal divine love. Fr. Kolbe personalized this truth, when he wrote, "Even when I did not yet exist, You already loved me, and by the very fact that You loved me, O Good God, You called me from nothing into existence."[50]

While we are each given our own proper existence, it is given to us for the sake of loving God, our happiness. Just as the Trinity is an eternal loving communion, so our existence – a participation in this one act – seeks communion. "From God we left and to God we tend by nature. This is a good example of the universal law of action and reaction, equal and opposite."[51] This "universal law" is a recurring theme in Kolbean teaching: our human action is a reaction to God's love.

Fr. Kolbe reminds us that, while every creature lives in this love and tends toward God, it belongs to man alone to intentionally participate in this response. In fact, "only man[52] (not always and not in everything) exchanges in an imperfect way this Divine love with love."[53] While by nature man tends toward God and final beatitude, we maintain a freedom of will to refuse the love of God. Therefore the reaction is not an inescapable law of physics. Man's happiness depends on whether he reacts in union with God as good or against it. In other words, it may be a reaction towards love, or it may be a reaction against love. Because man is free to more or less respond to the love of God, there are varying degrees of divine likeness among "the sons of God and men, the members of Christ." The most perfect, of course, is the Immaculata, full of grace.[54]

In the Immaculata's response to God and Christ's response to the Father, we discover the secret for making our response a true reaction of love. We must also repeat "Fiat," by uniting our will with their will. In this way man is united to Christ and able to offer a truly equal and opposite reaction to the one loving Trinity. It is equal in that man is united to the Will of God, and it is opposite as returning to the Trinity what came from the Trinity. Not only the ultimate end of man, but also the intermediate goals and in general every healthy activity has its principle in this love.[55] Therefore, human activity is essentially good, and to be otherwise is an unnatural deficiency. "Man was created for work."[56]

Our happiness lies in sanctity, and sanctity consists in the imitation of Christ. This has been discussed primarily in the need for supernatural obedience. However, the teaching on action and reaction manifests with even greater precision the participation in the divine life that is the consequence of this union of the wills. It is exclusively through the imitation of Christ that we are "divinized" and our likeness perfected. As St. Francis took up the Gospels and lived them literally, so St. Maximilian sought spiritually to imitate his Savior in everything. Love of the Immaculata was not an exception.

This love for the Immaculata was formalized in the total consecration. From the foundation of the Militia of the Immaculata many persons (including fellow friars and his own brother)[57] were uncomfortable with the totality and the passion with which Fr. Kolbe loved, honored, and praised the Immaculata.

In line with his desire to imitate Christ in all things, Fr. Kolbe's recurring, simple encouragement and admonition was this:

> Do not be afraid to love the Immaculata too much, ... we will never love Her the way that Jesus loved Her. All our sanctity consists in the imitation of Jesus. Whoever draws near to Her, also draws near to God, only he takes a shorter, more secure, easier road.[58]

> My dear Sons, if you desire to live and die happy, seek to deepen the filial love towards our best and heavenly Mother. Jesus was the first to honor Her as His Mother; following the commandment: "Honor your father and your mother."[59]

In other words, Christ was the first to be consecrated to Our Lady – to entrust Himself entirely to Her for the fulfillment of God's plan of redemption. While loving the Immaculata with the same kind of love that Jesus loved is impossible for mere humans, we may strive to love Her in imitation of our God. Similarly, it is impossible to love Jesus in the same way that the Immaculata loves Jesus, but we must strive for this as a path to perfection. This love is an active love because the Immaculata plays a particular role in the action and reaction between the Trinity and creation.

"The Immaculata's only desire is to raise the level of our spiritual life to the heights of holiness."[60] However, it is not God's will that She accomplishes this apostolic project alone, but rather it is Their desire to involve us in this activity. This is why it is essential to offer oneself totally to the Immaculata, so that She can use us as "instruments" for the sanctification of the world. In this way, even our most mundane activities become apostolic in nature.[61] There is a genuine exchange of love between humanity and the Holy Trinity. Continuing in imitation of Christ, however, this love is not stagnant, but creative. "When the fire of love ignites, it cannot find room in the limits of the heart, but goes forth and enflames, devours, and absorbs other hearts. It conquers always more numerous souls to its own ideal, the Immaculata."[62]

Love is in the will, and therefore great deeds are not necessary, only great love.[63] One becomes holy in ordinary everyday life. "That which has value, in fact, is not what we do, but the way, the intention, and the love with which we accomplish it. ... We must desire to please the Lord, in all things doing His Will: Carry with love the little everyday crosses, work with love, live with love ... Everyone can be and must be a missionary of this kind."[64] When one surrenders all to the Immaculata, everything he has and does belongs to Her. His actions become Her actions. And yet, because Her only desire is the conversion of souls, all Her actions are ordered to this end for the greatest glory of God. Thus the simple acts of love offered to the Immaculata become apostolic in nature. Fr. Kolbe reflects his heavenly friend, St. Therese of the Child Jesus, who wrote, "Since your soul is entirely delivered up to love, all your actions, even the most indifferent, are marked with this divine seal."[65]

This leads to the key characteristic: apostolic intent. Apostolic intent means to act with the intention of being united to the missionary work of the Church. It transforms even the most mundane activities into sources of evangelization. Fr. Kolbe desired the conversion of souls out of love for humanity; he knew that it is only in this way that one can arrive at authentic happiness and sublime holiness for the greatest glory of God.[66] This must be the animating force of our activity; we must work with all our strength for the salvation of souls.[67]

To the degree that we have surrendered to the Immaculata, to that degree will we be united to God, and to such a degree will our love be perfected. Accordingly, our apostolic activity will be great, even if our activity is not great in and of itself. Such surrender must be so total that it transforms the soul into a victim in imitation of our crucified Lord.

The holy Church teaches that all baptized persons share in the priestly ministry of Christ. This ministry is principally one of sacrificial offering. The words of St. Paul speak vividly of this priestly ministry, "I find my joy in the suffering I endure for you. In my own flesh I fill up what is lacking in the sufferings of Christ for the sake of his body, the Church."[68] The only way for our action to have redemptive value is to be fully united to Christ in the Paschal Mystery. Fr. Kolbe was well acquainted with the mystery and value of suffering. He suffered chronic tuberculosis, nervousness, severe headaches, and stomach ulcers. He experienced poor shelter in freezing temperatures and cramped quarters in sweltering heat. He experienced hunger near starvation, inadequate clothing, and the loss of loved ones. All this was experienced well before he endured the tortures of Auschwitz.

Still, he was happy to suffer for love of God, considering suffering willed out of love to be the pinnacle of one's gift of self, one's victimhood. The active dimension of this characteristic can be further clarified from insights of Fr. Luigi Faccenda. In his book, *One More Gift*, Fr. Faccenda defines *suffering willed out of love* as "accepting and loving sorrows and sufferings in our life, and making a total offering of ourselves to God for the redemption of the world through Mary."[69] Fr. Kolbe spoke of the infirmary as the most active and important apostolate in Niepokalanów. This was not because of the medics and nurses, but because of the patients. He believed that human weakness meant greater surrender, so that with St. Paul he could boast that his strength was in weakness joined to the power of the Crucified Savior.[70]

It is a common misconception that one must somehow forget oneself in order to please God, or that one must self-inflict suffering in order to overcome weakness or make reparation for sins. However, this contradicts the teaching of Fr. Kolbe and the Church. When Fr. Kolbe speaks of becoming a victim and suffering, he strikes a balance and enables one simultaneously to preserve both personal dignity and happiness in suffering. He asks: "What are we to do [in difficulties]?" and he responds,

36

"Trust in God... without limit." However, he does not allow for a passive acceptance. He asks, "So, we shouldn't worry about coming away or distancing ourselves from difficulty?" Encouragingly, he answers,

> Of course, one can and ought to do this; a lot depends on us. We need to do all that is possible to eliminate difficulty along the road of our life, but without restlessness, without anguish, and – even more – without desperate uncertainty. In fact, this state of soul does not help to resolve the difficulty, but makes us incapable of a wise, prudent, and rapid industriousness.[71]

Thus Fr. Kolbe insists on the two-fold reality of working to improve circumstances whenever possible (beginning with personal conversion), while accepting weaknesses and difficulties as opportunities to imitate and unite to Christ:

> Everybody admits that the road of our earthly existence is covered with small crosses. The acceptance of these crosses in the spirit of penance is the best field ... We are to fulfill our everyday duties and the will of God in every instant of our lives. The latter, which we must do perfectly in every action, word, or thought, demands giving up a lot of things we like. This is a plentiful source of penance.[72]

Ultimately, even acceptance is more active than passive. It is a willed decision to do penance – now understood as any obstacle or difficulty one faces – for love of God. When suffering is embraced for the sake of love, it purifies the individual and actually makes greater love possible. "From the lives of Jesus, Mary, and Fr. Kolbe we learn that suffering lived out of love, little by little, enables us to become more attentive to others' needs and to share in their sufferings. ... After love, suffering is the most universal and cohesive force."[73]

Giving oneself totally to the Immaculata as a victim with apostolic intent embraces Fr. Kolbe's specific apostolate and spirituality.

It manifests the possibility of receiving all necessary graces from the hands of the Immaculata, through the faithful accomplishment of one's ordinary duties. It sanctifies our actions that sanctify our lives, giving an apostolic dimension to every moment and task lived in love. Through such actions we become not only imitators of Jesus and Mary, but through Mary are transformed into Christ's likeness and united most intimately to His heart. "Only then, when we are nearly perfectly obedient to the Immaculata – we will become an exemplary instrument in Her apostolic hands. We will be apostles through the example of our daily life, apostles through our action."[74]

In order to thoroughly analyze the sanctifying nature of human activity according to Kolbean thought, it is necessary to consider what absorbed and motivated Fr. Kolbe's actions and teachings. How did he justify an intense and constant work load? How did he instruct the hundreds of thousands, both lay and cleric, who read *Rycerz Niepokalanej* and the various publications of Niepokalanów? In what direction did he lead his young pupils, seminarians and young friars, whether in Poland or Japan? The answer to these questions is found within the scope of the Militia of the Immaculata.

The Militia of the Immaculata was the field for most of Fr. Kolbe's active apostolate. He was very conscious of and moved by the duty and gift of the Church's missionary charism. He was further motivated by a desire to fight spiritually against Masonic blasphemies and the rise of false ideologies incarnated in Communism, Fascism, Socialism, and Nazism. Thus inspired, Fr. Kolbe founded the Militia of the Immaculata (here abbreviated MI) in Rome in 1917. Today, the MI is a public association of the faithful, thus publicly proclaimed as sharing in the mission of the universal Church. When its members fulfill the purpose of the MI they act in the name of the Church.[75] Belonging to a public association does not, by that fact, change the status of each individual member of the association. The laity remains lay, and clerics remain clerics. Therefore, the MI today still offers us both the spirit and teachings of a saintly priest from the early 20th century, and assures us that this same spirit and teaching is applicable to our lives. It remains a "global vision of Catholic life."[76]

> The nature of each thing is molded in conformity to the *end* for which it exists. For this reason, in order to know the nature of the MI, it is necessary to examine its end. Everything has a two-fold end: ultimate and immediate. ... The ultimate end of the MI is the *glory of God*. ... The immediate goal is the concern for the conversion of all non-Catholics...[77]

First of all, it is important to understand the meaning of "external glory." The glory of God is traditionally qualified as *external* or *internal*. The *internal glory* of God is the life of the Trinity, while *external glory* is the reflection of and participation in that glory by things created. Therefore, when creatures give glory to God and humans seek to glorify the Lord and do things for His greatest glory, there is an acknowledgment of participation as well as a plea to reflect the Holy Trinity.

Secondly, the immediate goal of "conversion of all non-Catholics" should be properly understood as the most perfect means of giving external glory to God, thus uniting immediate and ultimate ends. The reason for this is simply that no creation better reflects, draws souls into, or participates in the life of the Trinity than a soul in the state of grace. The greatest glory of God is a holy soul. For this reason, while the "conversion of all non-Catholics" is the immediate goal of Fr. Kolbe's apostolic initiative, he states over and over again that such conversion must begin with one's own personal sanctity. One example of his passion for evangelization through sanctification took place while Niepokalanów was experiencing apostolic success. Fr. Kolbe posed a question to his young friars:

> 'And now what must we do?' The friars, a little bit astounded, begin to ponder... A young man, full of energy,

answers in the heat of the excitement, 'Double the output!' A moment of silence follows. Fr. Kolbe, with bent head, seems to be absorbed in prayer. Then a shy voice whispers, *We will double the output if each one perfects himself.* The friars had never seen their Father as radiant as when he heard that answer.[78]

The nature of the MI, like all things, consists in matter and form. "The matter of the MI is the members. ... The form is the total, unlimited donation of oneself to the Holiest Virgin. ... She deigns to sanctify us and to unite others, through us, to God with the closest [*più stretto*] love possible."[79] While the tangible, evident substance of the MI is the members, that which specifies the movement is the total consecration to Mary under the title of the Immaculate Conception.

> The association is, first of all, 'I', that is to say 'Immaculatae' – of the Immaculata. The ideal of each of its members is to belong to the Immaculata, to be Her servant, son, slave of love, thing, property, in short, to belong to Her under whatever designation ... to belong to Her under every aspect for all life, death, and eternity. ... Behold the ideal: to become hers.

> A soul of this kind, in so far as he belongs to the Immaculata, conquers an always greater number of other souls for Her, by every legitimate means, and becomes not only property, but also knight of the Immaculata – 'M', that is to say, 'Miles.'[80]

The goal of the MI is so difficult to accomplish that, if one had to trust in only his energy, activity, and strength from nature, he could justly doubt the possibility of reaching it. Daily experience, in fact, teaches us that the enemies of the Church have more abundant natural means and often, according to the words of Christ, they are craftier than the sons of light.[81] Also, to obtain conversion and sanctification, grace is necessary, while corrupted nature is already inclined toward sin.

"Consequently, one can count only on help from heaven. And in this field the easiest and surest help, by the will of God, is the Most Holy Virgin Mary."[82]

If one has begun to grasp what Fr. Kolbe expects of the faithful, and in particular the Knights of the Immaculata, one may simultaneously begin to wonder whether meeting such expectations is even possible. When one hears the words, "Be perfect as your heavenly Father is perfect," there is often an attempt to equivocate the terms. Perfect? Impossible! Surely Scripture means something else! Surely Fr. Kolbe did not mean to give ourselves *totally* to the Immaculata! And yet, such is the case. Fr. Kolbe presents total consecration to the Immaculata as the surest and straightest means of reaching perfection. By the will of God, She is our hope for sanctification and happiness. She is the most excellent creation of the Holy Trinity. Her relationship to the Trinity is one of incredible intimacy, and this intimacy is the cause of our hope. Therefore, we will now look more deeply into the relationship between the Immaculate Conception and the Holy Trinity, and show the consequence of this relationship in our own intimate union with God.

The Immaculata is a created human person. She is the daughter of the Father. By nature She is exactly the same as every other human being (except Christ) who has walked and will walk on this earth. "By Herself She is nothing, like every other creature, but by the work of God She is the most perfect among creatures." Since all creatures are "like" God in varying degrees, it follows that "She is the most perfect likeness of the Divine Essence in a creature purely human."[83]

The Immaculata is the mother of the Son. Everything that She is, Her existence and every grace, has its source in this identity. This title is impossible for us to fully grasp because, while we may have an idea of what it means to be a mother, we can never grasp what it means to be God. We do know that this is both an act of humility on the part of God, submitting to a human person, and the exaltation of mankind as a mere human becomes the mother of a divine person.

She is the spouse of the Holy Spirit. Fr. Kolbe, as noted, was a faithful Franciscan. Accordingly, he did not look at the Immaculate Conception as much as free from sin, as full of grace. He understood the Immaculate Conception primarily positively, rather than negatively.[84] Fr. Kolbe was captivated by this mystery and spoke of it often. He had the intention of writing a book about the Immaculate Conception and the Holy Spirit, but was stopped by his arrest in February 1941. Fortunately, he had been taking notes, and we are left with a rich variety of texts on the subject. One such writing, quoted already above, is titled "Who are You?"[85] Taking a larger portion of the text will demonstrate this "positive" view of the Immaculate Conception and its key element: love.

> The Immaculata never had the least stain of sin, that is to say Her love was always total, without any defect. She loved God with all Her being. From the first instant of Her life, love united Her with God in such a perfect way that on the day of the annunciation the angel could address Her saying: 'Full of grace, the Lord is with you' (Lk 1:28).

> She is, therefore, creature of God, property of God, likeness of God, image of God, daughter of God, in the most perfect way possible for a mere human. ... She is an instrument of God in the perfect use of the faculties and privileges granted to Her, by accomplishing always and in everything, solely and exclusively the will of God, for the love of God one and three.

> This love of God reaches such heights that it produces divine fruits of love.

> Her union of love with God arrives to the point that She becomes the Mother of God. The Father entrusts to Her His own Son, the Son descends in Her womb, while the

Holy Spirit forms, from Her body, the most sacred body of Jesus.[86]

To be the Immaculate Conception is to be conceived in a state of grace, that is to be conceived full of grace. Since grace is the divine life in us, She more than anyone is united to God. She was conceived full of divine life. Furthermore, God is love. Therefore, the Immaculate Conception is full of God's love. And, properly speaking, the love of God is attributed to the Holy Spirit as the personification of the love between the Father and the Son. Therefore, "She is united in an ineffable way to the Holy Spirit, by the fact that She is His Spouse, but in an incomparably more perfect sense than this term can express in creatures."[87]

This union was not momentary, that is, a passing action of the Holy Spirit at the Annunciation. It began at Her conception and it continues for all eternity. Then, what kind of union is it? It is an interior union, the union of Her being with the Holy Spirit. The Holy Spirit dwells in Her. Of course, where the Holy Spirit is there also are the Father and Son. Therefore, this dwelling of the Holy Spirit in the Immaculate Conception means that the life of the Holy Trinity is present in Her. "The Holy Spirit is love in Her, the love of the Father and the Son, the love with which God loves Himself, the love of all the Holy Trinity."[88]

This union with the Holy Trinity, through the Holy Spirit, for the sake of the Incarnation, essentially defines the Immaculata. Fr. Kolbe means this literally, as he draws on this truth coupled with the Immaculata's announcement at Lourdes to say that the Immaculata actually is the Immaculate Conception, not just immaculately conceived. Fully analyzing this teaching, especially within the scope of this thesis, is impossible. However, for the sake of shedding light on our own union with God and the perfection of our action, it is important to at least lay out the teaching a little more fully.

Fr. Kolbe posits, "In created likenesses the union of love is the closest [più stretta]."[89] This is because the Holy Trinity is love. He then cites Genesis, "And the two shall become one" (Gen 2:24). He iterates that Christ confirmed this teaching when He said, "What God has joined together, no human being must separate" (Mt 19:6). The argument is that humans conceived with a corrupted nature are able to make a gift of self to another and share in the creation of life. In this loving, sacrificing union of persons they reflect the Holy Trinity (this is why marriage is a sacrament). Then how much more must the union of the Immaculata with the Holy Spirit be a reflection of the Holy Trinity? How much more fruitful? How much more should it be considered spousal?

After all, "In a way without paragon, more rigorous, more interior, more essential, the Holy Spirit lives in the soul of the Immaculata, in Her being.... ...and this from the first instant of Her existence and for life, that is always." Therefore, Fr. Kolbe does not hesitate to call Her "spouse" and "complement of the Most Holy Trinity."[90] So "spousal" is this union of love, that it gives the Immaculata Her name:

> If among creatures a spouse receives the name of her spouse, by the fact that she belongs to him, unites herself to him, makes herself like him, and united to him, becomes a factor in the creation of life, how much more the name of the Holy Spirit, "Immaculate Conception," is the name of She in whom He lives in a love that is fruitful in the entire supernatural economy.[91]

A name defines a person; this is the name that the Immaculata gave Herself at Lourdes. Fr. Kolbe understood this as defending and confirming the then recent proclamation of the Dogma of the Immaculate Conception. He also understood it to reveal the distinguishing essence of the Immaculata from all other created and uncreated persons.[92] Because of this intimate union between the Immaculata and the Holy Spirit, "the Holy Spirit ... does not exercise any influence on souls if not through

Her. For this reason, She became the Mediatrix of all graces, for this reason She is really the Mother of every divine grace."[93]

Christ is the source of all grace. Because He became flesh as fruit of the love of God and the Immaculata, every grace is fruit of this same union. "Every grace is fruit of the life of the Most Holy Trinity: the Father eternally generates the Son, while the Holy Spirit proceeds from the Father and the Son. ... Every grace comes from the Father, through the Son, by the Holy Spirit, ... Who forms souls [as He formed the Incarnate Word] in the likeness of the first born (primogenito), through and in the Immaculata."[94] This is the ultimate fruit of grace, to become like Christ, and it came to us through the Immaculata. So, it also returns "through the Holy Spirit and the Son, which is to say through the Immaculata and Jesus. This is the stupendous prototype of the principle of action and reaction, equal and opposite."[95]

Through the Immaculata, individual souls are given the divine life of sanctifying grace, and they are bound together by this life to form the whole Church. As Christ unites the Church as head of the Mystical Body, the Immaculata unites the Church as mother. "God is love, the Most Holy Trinity. Therefore, the mutual love of people that unites them to form a family is an authentic echo of divine love. That is, the love between a father, a mother, and a son." Still stronger is the "spiritual path of love that joins them in the intellect, the will, and being." Such is the case of the Immaculata, joined to the Holy Trinity. Such is the case of the mystical body, joined to the Holy Trinity, through Mary, through Christ. Such is the case of the individual members, washed in the waters of baptism and filled with the divine life, through Mary, through Christ. "The Holy Spirit through Her and in Her, communicates the supernatural life, the life of grace, the divine life, the participation in divine love, in divinity."[96]

The virgin womb of Mary became in time the place of the Incarnation. Jesus Christ, the sum of all created and divine perfection came to earth in the Immaculata by the power of the Holy Spirit. Therefore, in this union of love between the Immaculata and the Holy Spirit there was first of all the union of the two, with the Most Holy Trinity, and in the second place, the union of all creation. In this union, heaven was joined to earth, "all of heaven with all of earth, all of Uncreated Love with all of created love."[97] In Her the union of God with creation took place.[98] "At the Annunciation Mary responds to God's gift completely. She becomes the 'representative' of humanity in giving this perfect response of love to God Who waits to make a covenant with man. ... She is totally available to the action of the Spirit."[99]

Recalling that union with God is our final end as human beings, and therefore the source of our happiness and holiness pursued through obedience to His will as an act of love, it is now possible to see that the Immaculata accomplishes all this in a way superior to any other creature. "She is the highest perfection of all creation, Mother of God, the most divinized among creatures."[100] Therefore, in imitation of Christ, who lowered Himself from the heavens to be formed and nurtured in Her immaculate womb,

> We ought to be reborn according to the form of Jesus Christ. She must nourish the soul with the milk of Her grace, care for it lovingly, and teach it as She nourished, cared for, and educated Jesus. At Her knees the soul must learn to know and to love Jesus. From Her heart it must attain love towards Him, to love Him with Her heart and to become like Him through love.[101]

Only in becoming like Him and uniting oneself to Him will we fulfill our natural human desire for happiness. And, what is more, to the degree that we accomplish this, to that degree will we be happy and holy. Hence, the Immaculata is the purest and the happiest of all creation.

Fr. Kolbe states that Christ left two things upon the earth in order to transform us into Himself: the Holy Eucharist and His own mother.[102] The two are inseparable because She is the mother of the Eucharist and the instrument of its graces. Therefore, the Immaculata is truly and effectively our hope for happiness and holiness. She is our model and our mother. She is the mediatrix of all grace and the pinnacle of love between the Creator and the creature. This is why the total consecration to the Immaculata, the total surrender to Her for the salvation of souls and the greatest glory of God, is the specific means of Fr. Kolbe's teaching on holiness and happiness. Through Her we are caught up in a perfected reaction to God's love poured out on earth. With Her we are able to respond to the call to holiness with the words of Her Son, "Thy will be done." In Her we find the perfect balance, our hope for a life of union with God, beginning in this earthly life and culminating in eternal beatitude.

Before we proceed to the final stage of this thesis, namely defining the relationship between this union with God that is modeled in the Virgin Mary and the active life every human has or does experience, it is important to emphasize the centrality of the Incarnation. Our union with God occurs through the Immaculate Conception according to the will of God as a sign to us of our dignity and destiny. Our union with God is a direct result of His infinite mercy, of which She is the most perfect instrument because She immediately participates in its presence.

> Already there is a bridge toward the Most Sacred Heart of Jesus. Whoever falls in sin ... has a Mother given to us by God, a Mother that follows with a tender heart every action, word, and thought. She is not worried whether one is worthy of the grace of mercy. She is Mother only of mercy (Mother of Christ), and therefore runs quickly, even if not invoked, where there is the gravest misery of souls. However much the soul is disfigured by sin, so much more is divine mercy manifest.[103]

Every moment in union with the Immaculata, with the understanding that She is united to Jesus and Jesus is most perfectly united to the Father, consequently unites us with the

47

Holy Trinity.[104] So, we move forward confidently turned to the mediatrix of all grace and dependent on God's mercy as the possibility of our union with Him. Now, finally Fr. Kolbe's teaching on the nature of the relationship between union with God and action will be demonstrated. Fr. Kolbe insists that this relationship between a profound interior life and apostolic dynamism is the only true means to holiness and happiness.

Notes

44 "I admit that for a time, because of difficulties here, I was depressed, and I yearned for respite. ... Because alone we're so weak, and there're so many devils here who can't digest the fact that we've come this far, ..." Claude R. Foster, *Mary's Knight* (West Chester, PA: West Chester University Press, 2002), 381.

45 Kolbe, for an unpublished book, August 5-20, 1940, in *Scritti* sec. 1326. Note: Kolbe of course acknowledged the fall of creation with the fall of man. In this quote and similar texts he is speaking of the ontological goodness of being and not making reference to moral goodness.

46 Kolbe, "Chi è Dio?" *Rycerz Niepokalanej*, February 1923, 21-23. in *Scritti* sec. 1027.

47 Kolbe, "Immacolata," *Miles Immaculatae*, January-March 1938, 8-9. in *Scritti* sec. 1224.

48 Kolbe, Unpublished, Niepokalanów, end of 1937, in *Scritti* sec. 1282.

49 Duns Scotus, *Ord.* lib. III, d. 32, q. unica; ed. Vivès, XV, 433; translation in Wolter, "Primacy and Personality," 156-7. Cited by Pio Maria Hoffmann, "The 'Return' of the Primacy of Christ," (Master's Thesis, Saint Joseph's Seminary, Dunwoodie, 2007), 15.

50 Kolbe, "Chi ardirebbe supporre?...," *Rycerz Niepokalanej*, November 1929, 327-329. in *Scritti* sec. 1145.

51 Kolbe, "Nella notte tra il 13 e il 14 aprile," *Rycerz Niepokalanej*, June 1926, 168-171. in *Scritti* sec. 1124.

52 In this text Fr. Kolbe is speaking specifically about earthly creatures (creature terrestri) and so does not take into consideration angels. Because this thesis pertains to man's life with God, this question will not be addressed. Let it suffice to state that the angels, as creation, are part of the "action and reaction" between God and his creation. Furthermore, they too fall short of the perfection of the Immaculata, who is the most perfect creation whether terrestrial or angelic.

53 Kolbe, for an unpublished book, Niepokalanów, August 5-20, 1940, in *Scritti* sec. 1326.

54 Kolbe, Unpublished, Niepokalanów, end of 1937, in *Scritti* sec. 1282.

55 Cf. Kolbe, Unpublished, Niepokalanów, end of 1937, in *Scritti* sec. 1283 and sec. 1284.

56 Kolbe, Spiritual Exercises, Krakow, September-October 1912, in *Scritti* sec. 962.

57 Cf. Foster, *Mary's Knight*, 165, 314, 315.

58 Kolbe to p. Floriano Koziura, Mugenzai no Sono, November 2, 1933, in *Scritti* sec. 542.

59 Kolbe to seminaristi di prima Liceo, Zakopane, October 14, 1937, in *Scritti* sec. 751.

60 Kolbe, "La M.I.," *Rycerz Niepokalanej*, December 1937, 357-358. in *Scritti* sec. 1220.

61 Kolbe, "Poveretti...," *Rycerz Niepokalanej*, January 1926, 2-7. in *Scritti* sec. 1113.

62 Kolbe, for an unpublished book, Niepokalanów or Zakopane, 1939, in *Scritti* sec. 1325.

63 Kolbe, Personal Notes, Niepokalanów, January 6, 1937, in *Scritti* sec. 1354.

64 Kolbe, Unpublished, aboard the ship 'Angkor,' July 1932, in *Scritti* sec. 1263.

65 Thèrése de Lisieux, *Story of a Soul* (Public Domain Books, 2009), Kindle Edition, l. 2521.

66 Kolbe, for an unpublished book, Niepokalanów or Zakopane, 1939, in *Scritti* sec. 1325.

67 Kolbe to lettori di Kronika Seraficka, Mugenzai no Sono, September 25, 1931, in *Scritti* sec. 370.

68 Col 1:24 (NAB).

69 Faccenda, *One More Gift* (1990; repr., West Covina, CA: Immaculata Press, 1991), 77.

70 2 Cor 12:9-10, "My grace is sufficient for you, for power is made perfect in weakness. I will rather boast most gladly of my weaknesses, in order that the power of Christ may dwell with me. Therefore, I am content with weaknesses, insults, hardships, persecutions, and constraints, for the sake of Christ; for when I am weak, then I am strong."

71 Kolbe, Unpublished, Mugenzai no Sono, 1932-1933, in *Scritti* sec. 1264.

72 Kolbe, Unpublished, Niepokalanów, 1940, in *Scritti* sec. 1303.

73 Faccenda, *One More Gift*, 79.

74 Kolbe, "La M.I.".

75 See "General Statutes of the Militia of the Immaculate," art. 1: "The Militia of the Immaculate, founded in Rome by St. Maximilian Kolbe on 16 October 1917 with the Latin name *Militia Immaculatae* (*M.I.*), is a public association of the faithful ... governed by the norms of canons 312-320 of the CJC, ..."

76 "General Statutes of the Militia of the Immaculate," art. 3. Cf. Kolbe, *Scritti* sec. 1220.

77 Kolbe, Unpublished, Krakow, November 15, 1919, in *Scritti* sec. 1248.

78 Faccenda, *Symbiosis*, 54.

79 Kolbe, Unpublished, Krakow, November 15, 1919, in *Scritti* sec. 1248.

80 Kolbe, "M.I.," *Rycerz Niepokalanej*, December 1936, 356-357. in *Scritti* sec. 1211.

81 Lk 16:8.

82 Kolbe, "La prima condizione," *Rycerz Niepokalanej*, May 1922, 102. in *Scritti* sec. 1007.

83 Kolbe, for an unpublished book, Niepokalanów, after August 1940, in *Scritti* sec. 1320.

84 See Faccenda, "Father Kolbe, the Immaculata, and the Most Holy Trinity," 8-15.

85 Foster, *Mary's Knight,* 649-650.

86 Kolbe, for an unpublished book, Niepokalanów, after August 1940, in *Scritti* sec. 1320.

87 Kolbe, for an unpublished book, Niepokalanów, February 17, 1941, in *Scritti* sec. 1318.

88 Ibid.

89 Ibid.

90 Ibid.

91 Ibid.

92 Kolbe, for an unpublished book, Niepokalanów, August 5-20, 1940, in *Scritti* sec. 1319.

93 Kolbe, "Immacolata," *Miles Immaculatae*, January-March 1938, 8-9. in *Scritti* sec. 1224.

94 Kolbe, Unpublished, Niepokalanów, 1940 in *Scritti* sec. 1296.

95 Kolbe to fr. Salesio Mikolajczyk, Nagasaki, July 28, 1935, in *Scritti* sec. 634.

96 Kolbe, for an unpublished book, Niepokalanów, August 5-20, 1940, in *Scritti* sec. 1326.

97 Kolbe, for an unpublished book, Niepokalanów, February 17, 1941, in *Scritti* sec. 1318.

98 Kolbe, for an unpublished book, Niepokalanów, August 5-20, 1940, in *Scritti* sec. 1310.

99 Faccenda, "Father Kolbe, the Immaculata, and the Most Holy Trinity," 13.

100 Kolbe, for an unpublished book, Niepokalanów or Zakopane, 1939, in *Scritti* sec. 1325.

101 Kolbe, Unpublished, Niepokalanów 1940, in *Scritti* sec. 1295.

102 Kolbe, Unpublished, Niepokalanów 1940, in *Scritti* sec. 1296.

103 Kolbe, "Attraverso l'Immacolata al sacratissimo Cuore di Gesù," *Rycerz Niepokalanej*, June 1925, 130-132. in *Scritti* sec. 1094.

104 Kolbe, Unpublished, Niepokalanów, end of 1937, in *Scritti* sec. 1284.

Within the human heart there is a desire for happiness that one experiences as a yearning for wholeness. It is common to hear (and utter) phrases such as "Life is hard!" and "Why me?" It is common to project our problems onto situations and claim that religion is just too hard. After all "little sins are OK, because they don't hurt anyone anyway!" There arises in the human person a dichotomy between the interior, higher part of man, and the active, external part of him. If a resolution is not found, happiness is lost. On the other hand, if a resolution can be found, then happiness in this life is possible. Society throws around phrases such as "well-being" and "balanced life," but only in synchronizing our interior and external life will we ever be able to achieve real balance and well-being.

It has been determined that man is destined for union with God. This remarkable truth has its source in our nature as *imago Dei*. Created in His image we tend toward wholeness and perfection by perfecting that image within us, by becoming like Him. Such is possible through the actual indwelling of the divine life within us, commonly called grace. Grace is engendered in us by the power of the Holy Spirit through the Immaculata. Accordingly, our human nature is intended to be united to God by His merciful decree. Because the life of grace begins in this life, then our union with God also begins in this life.

This is our interior life, the life of God within us. To the degree that we foster an intimate relationship with that divine presence, allowing Our Lady to nurture and protect us, to that degree will the life of God be effective in us. This divine life, when nurtured properly, does not remain entrapped within an individual interior life, but rather draws the person into God's own mission. God is love. God is creative. Love is creative. Therefore, that same divine love transforms us into an adopted child of God. To the degree that we are docile to this grace, reacting towards love, this same divine love transforms souls around us. This is love; love for God everywhere and in every person. This is the powerful binding force that unites us first individually to our Creator, and then to one another in His Mystical Body.

Fr. Kolbe expresses these sentiments over and over again. In the previous parts of this thesis, we have seen each piece in detail, and now the larger vision. Union with God, which is contemplation, and action are compatible and inseparable. It is impossible to separate union with God from action, just as it is impossible to separate God from His creation. Wherever the interior life is healthy, the active life is loving, and together they are sanctifying. There is a symbiosis between contemplation and action, that is, a mutually beneficial relationship. If one were to be neglected and avoided the other would cease to exist. Without each, man cannot be fully human, and therefore neither fully happy, because he cannot be perfected in his dignity as image of God.

Fr. Kolbe presents this teaching with clarity. Though not explicitly in these terms, if one gathers even just the well known facts of his life, the spirit that has thus far been laid out, and various essential writings with recurring themes, it is evident that Fr. Kolbe lived the symbiosis of contemplation and action. He considered it the natural means for our happiness and salvation. In other words, we are called by God's holy will to be united to Him beginning in this life. We are called to live a fully human existence defined by loving surrender to Our Lord and Savior. Dependent on the framework that has thus far been laid out, the remaining part of this thesis will draw from one key text, cited by several authors[106] to be significant of contemplation and action in Kolbean thought. Subsequently each part will be explained, thus revealing why such a reading is in fact conducive to the thought of Fr. Kolbe.

Fr. Kolbe was struck by a nearly insatiable desire to save souls; his passion for the apostolate knew no bounds. He uses terms such as "fire," "heart," "totality," "victim," and "property," in order to express the radicalness and urgency of the apostolic activity. Yet, he was forced to spiritually and practically consider what makes apostolic activity fruitful. He was faced with the reality that some apostolates were sterile, lifeless, while his own was flourishing beyond everyone's (but his own) imagination. The difference, ultimately, was that God's work bears fruit and man's work (alone) does not. What is needed is a loving union with God that overflows into the love of neighbor. God loving in you, in fact, means that even one's actions become supernatural, even mystical. God's love in the human heart can reach such depth as to overpower the basic human inclination to preserve one's life. God's love empowers man to imitate Christ unto giving one's life out of love.

The first text we will analyze comes from an article Fr. Kolbe wrote in response to the "sterility" of some apostolic action. He applies his reflection to the life of the Militia of the Immaculata. The second text is actually a continuation, but occurs in another equally pertinent writing. The text is the metaphor of the vine and the branches, often quoted, but the insight which Fr. Kolbe lends is astounding.

The first verse is preceded by a sentence we have already quoted, but we repeat here in order to set the context: "Catholic action is a sublime work, so sublime, it is collaboration (if it is licit to express it like this) with God in the perfection, sanctification, and happiness of men." Fr. Kolbe continues:

> But, with regard to this work the Savior himself said expressly to the apostles: "Remain in me, as I remain in you. Just as a branch cannot bear fruit unless it remains on the vine, so neither can you unless you remain in me. I am the vine, you are the branches. Whoever remains in me and I in him will bear much fruit, because *without me you can do nothing*" (Jn 15:4-6).[107]

Fr. Kolbe directly connects a fruitful active life and union with God. This union is nothing superficial, a following from several feet behind, or even hand in hand. This union is the entrance into the life of the Trinity by remaining in Christ and allowing Him to remain in us. We know that this is possible, though always mysterious, through grace. Essentially, Fr. Kolbe is awakening the awareness of the reality of grace as the divine life in us. This affirms and promotes the age-old teaching of the Church on nature and grace. That grace perfects nature is often forgotten in man's desire to sanctify and discover happiness by his own power and on his own terms. The sheer impossibility of this is emphasized in Fr. Kolbe's words closing this paragraph: "The Lord does not say you cannot do 'many things', but 'nothing' - absolutely nothing."

Another essential element of the personal intimacy of this union is that Christ is the vine, and we are the branches. Therefore, while all depends on Him, we do have an existence in a way our own. We have not lost our individuality, or personality; we discover and perfect it through union with Him. Man's perfection is not an unnatural change, but a supernatural transformation.

The fruit is the effect of this union. The first fruits that Fr. Kolbe describes man seeking are perfection, sanctification, and happiness. We know that such is found in imitation of Christ, and indeed the branches do grow in "imitation" of the vine. They are infinitely more fragile, weak, and incapable of existence without the vine, but they are also similar to the vine as being nourished by the same source and collaborating to bring fruit upon the earth. Therefore, every fruit of our activity depends on union with Christ. Furthermore, we can do all things in Christ who strengthens us, and add with Fr. Kolbe, "through the Immaculata."[108]

That this fruit depends primarily on our union with God through the Immaculata confirms the primacy of the interior life and the first goal of the Militia of the Immaculata, that is, the need for personal sanctification. According to Fr. Kolbe, this is of utmost importance.[109] In 1920 he took note: "Interior life: dedicate oneself completely to oneself, so that one can give oneself completely to all (*Vita interiore: 'Totus primo sibi et sic totus omnibus'*)"[110] Accordingly, we must develop our personal love for the Savior, specifically by entering into "our interior desert to prepare ourselves for the public life."[111] This is clearly an allusion to Christ, once again beckoning us to imitate Him in all things. If we do, than the union that is possible will certainly defy our greatest expectations. It leads to a union of spousal intimacy:

> In imitation of this first Son of God, of the infinite Man-God, we must be formed from now on into sons of God; reproducing the image of the Man-God, imitating Christ the Lord souls will tend toward sanctity; to the degree that one exactly reproduces in himself the image of Christ, to that degree he draws near to divinity, is 'divinized,' becomes man-God. It is the marriage of the soul [sposalizio dell'anima] with Christ, to be in His likeness and for divine action.[112]

This union is what makes our action truly "sublime" or rather "divine," not by our own efforts, but specifically through surrender to the life of God within us. This spousal love is a reflection and an invitation into the life of the Trinity, which is perfect love. It is a reflection and invitation into the love that the Immaculata has for the Holy Trinity. We love with Her heart the Father, Son, and Holy Spirit and are moved by Her to please Them. "Whoever consecrates themselves to Her in a truly perfect way has already reached sanctity, and to the degree that one perfectly lets themselves be led by Her in the interior life (spiritual) and the exterior life (apostolic activity), to that degree does one participate in Her sanctity."[113] We share in Her union with the Trinity, in Her spousal relationship, and in Her work and mission.

As a result, the interior life must be enflamed by the love of God, which does not permit us to flee from life's obstacles or be cut-off from our difficulties and tribulations. Duties and responsibilities are a part of our normal, everyday human activity.

Love "urges us more every day to conquer our own heart for the Immaculata."[114] Furthermore, the extent of our surrender ultimately demonstrates our own love of God, and we will one day be judged by how we loved. The Bible verse that Fr. Kolbe quoted above continues: "Anyone who does not remain in me will be thrown out like a branch and wither; people will gather them and throw them into a fire and they will be burned."[115]

Fr. Kolbe's love for the truth moves him to be blunt when insisting on personal union with God. In synchrony with Fr. Kolbe's teaching that all things tend toward perfection, and that God is all good, he looks to eternal life to satisfy and complete all that is imperfect in this life. Among these things is justice, which will be manifested by our (personal) commitment to heaven or hell:[116]

> If heaven and hell do not exist, everyone ought to know the truth. But if they do exist, well then, this must also have value for everyone because before God every man is equal. If God exists, a God infinitely perfect, then He must be infinitely wise, good, and just; therefore, without any exception, after death each one will give account to Him of each thought, word, and action. Each one will receive the most just reward or the greatest punishment.[117]

One, however, must not be intimidated by the truth. God is truth, and also the way, and the life. God is good and wise, and has promised: "If you remain in me and my words remain in you, ask for whatever you want and it will be done for you. By this is my Father glorified, that you bear much fruit and become my disciples."[118] We put our faith in the mercy of God, knowing that He is the "best Father" and "desires to give us *all* that we need."[119] So great is the love of the Creator for us that, though He demands that we become like little children in order to enter paradise, likewise He knows that every child needs a mother.

Fr. Kolbe thus addresses the Lord, "Your goodness and mercy, therefore, have created for us a Mother, the personification of

Your goodness and infinite love, ... Who, then, cannot reach paradise?"[120] Sin and its consequences are not due to a lack on the part of God or sheer incapability on the part of man, but rather in trusting our strength more than the mercy of God. We doubt the power of His love, and the mediation of the Immaculata. The importance of asking, prayer is underlined and followed by the counsel to become a disciple, a follower, which implies action. Prayer leads to action.

Union with God is possible, but not guaranteed. Happily, Fr. Kolbe continues to offer insight into the nature of this loving union as we continue with the text of the vine and the branches: "As the Father loves me, so I also love you. Remain in my love." We know that all things come to us from the Father, through Christ, and this includes the love of the Trinity. This love, as the binding force between us and God, is so incomprehensible because it makes us God's "equals."[121] These words are shocking, to be sure, but the Word of God verifies that He "did not regard equality with God something to be grasped. Rather, He emptied himself, taking the form of a slave, coming in human likeness; and found human in appearance, He humbled himself, becoming obedient to death, even death on a cross."[122] Fr. Kolbe invites us to remember well that Jesus died for each one of us without any exception.

And yet, to remain in this love, as commanded by the Lord, requires a response on our part. Continuing the analysis of the vine and the branches we discover the response as well as the bridge towards action: "If you keep my commandments, you will remain in my love, just as I have kept my Father's commandments and remain in His love." Therefore, love not only binds us to the Lord, but is directly related to keeping the commandments. This is another way of saying that love is doing the will of God. It is His will that we be sanctified by Christ, who Has redeemed us at a dear price with His death on the cross. "This ought to be our *sublime ideal of life*: everything to bring the greatest possible joy to the Sacred Heart."[123] Taking example from this profound love of Christ shown by His obedience unto death, and wishing to imitate Christ always more perfectly, Fr. Kolbe connects love and the will, interior life and action, when he says, "Love, that is, *unlimited love* towards our best Father, is shown through obedience."[124] Furthermore, it is impossible for love to cause misery (no matter how faint that love might be), because love is union with God.

Heaven is the perfection of love, but such joy can begin here on this earth. It is a friendship so exalted that it defies explanation and understanding, except by those who have experienced it: "Indeed, true friendship savors happiness in suffering for the person loved. Therefore, there is nothing strange in that the saints found their paradise here on earth, not in what pleased them, nor in honors, and not in riches, but in poverty, humiliation, and suffering accepted for love of God."[125] Considering this we will better understand the last three sentences of the vine and the branches.

"I have told you this so that my joy may be in you and your joy may be complete. This is my commandment: love one another as I love you." Having shown the primacy of the interior life and the possibility and nature of union with God, finally it is shown first of all that our human end is achieved in this union. Union with God is our happiness. This is not a fleeting happiness, but a complete joy, so complete that it is the joy of the Trinity.

Remember that the nature of the Trinity is an eternal, loving, gift of self between the three persons of the Trinity. It is an eternal, joyful, loving relationship. All that has been said finds its source and summit in this joyful loving relationship. In this scripture passage, Christ promises us that if we imitate Him, we will have that same love. Just as the love of the Trinity does not remain contained, but pours forth in creation, so our love cannot remain within ourselves. These words of Fr. Kolbe reaffirm that this is an authentic interpretation of his thought: "The love of God is the only source of authentic and sincere love towards neighbor... (thus) humanity will draw near, as much as it is possible on this earth, to happiness, in anticipation of that happiness towards which each one of us naturally tends already, that is to say to happiness without limit, in God, in heaven."[126]

Two necessary effects of this union with God are the love of and the union with our neighbor. The two cannot be divided, as love is a unifying force. It builds up and gives peace where otherwise there is separation, division, and destruction.[127]

> It is evident that Jesus deeply desired that a sincere love reign among men. The apostles understood well Jesus' desire. This is why St. Peter writes in a letter, 'Above all, let your love for one another be intense, because love covers a multitude of sins,' (1 Pt 4:8) ... and in his first letter St. John writes, 'Beloved, let us love one another, because love is of God; everyone who loves is begotten by God and knows God' (1 Jn 4:7).[128]

Therefore, while our "first concern" is our own union with God, "the commitment to the sanctification of others must come from a super-abundant love for Jesus."[129]

Fr. Kolbe's hope and trust was in the Immaculata. He knew that the most perfect way to love Christ, even "super-abundantly," was through and with the Immaculata. In order to maximize the number of souls reached, and thus increase the glory of God, it is necessary to "belong every day more to the Immaculata; in Her and through Her to Jesus; and in Him and through Him to the Heavenly Father; under every aspect. And consecrate [your] entire life to this: to carry this happiness to your neighbor."[130]

The more one deepens his love and veneration for the Immaculata, the more souls one conquers for Her and through Her for Christ, who loved us unto death on the cross. In His self-offering, Christ shows us the greatest love, love to the maximum because it is an "active love." If one moves towards this kind of love, towards the Sacred Heart of Jesus, he unites himself to Christ in the most perfect way possible.[131]

> In the end, *love your neighbor*. Love your neighbor, but not because he is 'nice', useful, rich, influential or only

because he gives recognition. These are very unworthy motives, unworthy of a knight of the Immaculata. Authentic love elevates one above creation and immerses him in God: in Him, for Him, and through Him love everyone, good and bad, friend and enemy. Extend a hand full of love to everyone, pray for everyone, suffer for everyone, wish everyone well, desire everyone's happiness because it is God who wants it!...[132]

We are called to this heroic charity, which is only possible if God acts in us and for us. It is a love that consists in the "union with Jesus by means of an unlimited loving friendship, and through this, union with our neighbors."[133] We have seen what Fr. Kolbe says of friendship, and we know what Christ thought of friendship. And so it is just that the very pinnacle of union with God in action is expressed in the words spoken by our Lord: "No one has greater love than this, to lay down one's life for one's friends."[134]

Yes, it is possible to be united to God in action. This is our sanctification, our happiness, the full flourishing of our humanity. Who of us will be victorious? "Only the one who in prayer to the Immaculata, whether formed on his lips or hidden ... in a heart purified and on fire with God's love, is willing to do all in his power through the Immaculata to win as many souls as possible for God, freeing them from the shackles of evil and making them happy in Him."[135] The truly happy man, therefore, is he who lives the awesome symbiosis of contemplation and action. Christ, the Immaculata, and finally St. Maximilian Kolbe have shown us the way.

105 As mentioned at the beginning of this thesis, the idea (more than the content) for this thesis was taken from Fr. Luigi Faccenda's work: *Symbiosis: Contemplation and Action.* This section shares the title of this book as the straightforward explanation for the relationship this thesis is demonstrating between contemplation and action. Proper footnotes attribute to Fr. Faccenda any idea or direct quote that is taken from this or any of his writings.

106 See in particular Fr. Faccenda and Fr. Louvencourt.

107 Kolbe, "Il segreto del successo nell'azione cattolica," *Rycerz Niepokalanej,* October 1924, 193-194. in *Scritti* sec. 1071.

108 Kolbe, Spiritual Exercises, Krakow, February 17-22, 1920, in *Scritti* sec. 971.

109 Kolbe, Meditations, Rome, January-March 1919, in *Scritti* sec. 987 F.

110 Kolbe, Spiritual Exercises, Krakow, February 17-22, 1920, in *Scritti* sec. 971.

111 Kolbe, Meditations, Rome, January-March 1919.

112 Kolbe, Unpublished, Niepokalanów, December 1940, in *Scritti* sec. 1295.

113 Kolbe to fr. Cornelio Czupryk, Mugenzai no Sono, Japan, January 18, 1932, in *Scritti* sec. 389.

114 Kolbe, Spiritual Exercises, Rome, October 21, 1913 and following, in *Scritti* sec. 963.

115 Jn 15:6.

116 Kolbe, "Capodanno," *Mugenzai no Seibo no Kishi,* January 1934, 2-4. in *Scritti* sec. 1176.

117 Kolbe, Unpublished, Mugenzai no Sono, toward the end of 1933, in *Scritti* sec. 1268.

118 Jn 15:7-8.

119 Kolbe, "Il segreto della forza e della potenza," *Rycerz Niepokalanej,* September 1925, 225-227. in *Scritti* sec. 1100.

120 Kolbe, "Chi ardirebbe supporre?...," *Rycerz Niepokalanej,* November 1929, 327-329. in *Scritti* sec. 1145.

121 CCC, 460: "The Word became flesh to make us *'partakers of the divine nature'* (2 Pt 1:4): 'For this is why the Word became man, and the Son of God became the Son of man: so that man, by entering into communion with the Word and thus receiving divine sonship, might become a son of God' (St. Irenaeus, *Adv. haeres.* 3, 19, 1: PG 7/1, 939). 'For the Son of God became man so that we might become God' (St. Athanasius, *De inc.* 54, 3: PG 25, 192B). 'The only-begotten Son of God, wanting to make us sharers in his divinity, assumed our nature, so that he, made man, might make men gods'" (St. Thomas Aquinas, *Opusc.* 57, 1-4).

122 Phil 2:6 (Cf. Kolbe, *Scritti* sec. 908).

123 Kolbe to fr. Alfonso Kolbe, Rome, April 21, 1919, in *Scritti* sec. 25.

124 Ibid.

125 Kolbe, "Una religione difficile," *Rycerz Niepokalanej*, November 1934, 327. in *Scritti* sec. 1190.

126 Kolbe, "La Regina della Polonia," *Rycerz Niepokalanej*, May 1925, 97-102. in *Scritti* sec. 1093.

127 Kolbe, "La religione dell'amore," *Mugenzai no Seibo no Kishi*, March 1936, 2ff. in *Scritti* sec. 1205.

128 Ibid.

129 Kolbe, Meditations, Rome, January-March 1919, in *Scritti* sec. 987 F.

130 Kolbe, Personal Notes, Niepokalanów, June 17, 1938, in *Scritti* sec. 1362.

131 Kolbe, "Attraverso l'Immacolata al sacratissimo Cuore di Gesù".

132 Kolbe, "La nostra tattica," *Rycerz Niepokalanej*, November 1925, 217-218. in *Scritti* sec. 1075.

133 Kolbe, Meditations, Rome, January-March 1919, in *Scritti* sec. 987 F.

134 Jn 15:13. Cf. John Paul II, "Homily given at the canonization of Maximilian Kolbe," October 10, 1982.

135 Kolbe, *Rycerz Niepokalanej*, quoted in *Symbiosis*, 40.

Conclusion

All men are created in the image and likeness of God. We come from the love of the Trinity and are ordered to be united to the Father, Son, and Holy Spirit. This creates in man, throughout his sojourn on earth, a yearning for wholeness and completion that will only be perfected in the life to come. Man, corrupted by original sin and walking in a vale of tears, does not always realize that he is in search of God. Man only knows that he wants to be happy. Still, there are many who in fact do know God, and even know that God is love and the source of happiness, and yet these are often plagued by a relentless lack of peace and joy. One wonders if happiness is an illusion, if union with God is just something that needs to be put off until we "get through" this life. One wonders if this life of apparently increasing chaos is just an obstacle to our happiness with all its activity and monotonous daily duties.

This thesis has recognized this dilemma of man, and has shown that according to St. Maximilian Kolbe happiness is possible, to some degree, in this life through living a life of contemplation and action. Action is not an impediment to union with God, and union with God is not an impediment to action. Rather, they are mutually beneficial to the other, inseparable, and essential to a wholly human, happy life.

While this relationship is symbiotic, it is recognized that primacy belongs to the interior life. It is within the interior life, specifically in the union of the will of man with the will of God, that this union takes place. The surrendering of the will to God is an offering of our freedom, essentially the only thing that we can offer. The union of the wills conforms us to Christ, whom we imitate in obedience. Fr. Kolbe calls this surrender to and for the one you love authentic friendship. In imitation of Christ, this surrender of the will becomes an active love as one ultimately – in a red or white martyrdom – gives his life for his friends, that is, for his fellow man.

Such heroism is impossible without the divine life that comes to us as grace through the Immaculate Conception. All grace comes to us through Her, instrument of God's unfathomable mercy, as Christ the source of all grace came to us through Her by the power of the Holy Spirit. It was the love of the Immaculata for God and of God for the Immaculata that formed the Incarnation in Her womb. Through Her we are reborn into an always more perfect image of this Incarnation, united to Christ and through Christ to God the Father. Such intimacy with the Holy Trinity bears the fruit of personal sanctification, which is our primary concern, and participating in the creative love of the Trinity bears the fruit of drawing others to the happiness that is union with God. Our collaboration with this divine grace, the fruit of our action, is made always more perfect and effective to the degree that we live our total consecration to the Immaculata.

Above all prayer is effective in obtaining the grace of conversion, whether initial justification or constant transformation into Christ. Grace strengthens the will and illumines the intellect, opening the way to conversion. Transformation into Christ is a way of defining a constantly deepening union with God through love. Love is creative, and therefore love is active. When our actions, from the most monotonously trivial to the most heroic are done in this love – for, with, and in the Immaculata – they become a participation in the redeeming act of Christ. It does not essentially matter what one does, only how one does it. Love is the only standard by which we will be judged; it is the only measure of true happiness.

Therefore, amid trials and sufferings, joys and victories, friends and enemies, births and deaths, we turn toward the Immaculata and go forward with absolute confidence in the love of God that comes to us through Her. We work and study, pray and play with hands, feet, and mind dedicated to His glory and our hearts enflamed with love, united to the Holy Trinity in every place and in every moment. This is the ideal of

Christ: to love one another as He has loved us. He belonged to the Immaculata and gave Himself up for us, in obedience to the Father, as a victim for the salvation and happiness of our souls. The ideal of Fr. Kolbe, proposed in this thesis as the symbiosis between contemplation and action, therefore takes on a brilliant and evangelical light: Belong to the Immaculata as a victim with apostolic intent. This is our ideal. This is our happiness.

Appendix

Adapted from "Fr. Kolbe and Fr. Faccenda: Spiritual Bond," by Rossella Bignami, Fr. Kolbe Missionary of the Immaculata

Fr. Luigi Faccenda and Fr. Maximilian Kolbe walked the earth at the same time in history. They never met, but their lives were affected by the same World Wars. Their countries were on different sides of World War II, that war that pitted human against human, Christian against Christian in an unprecedented bath of blood-shed. It was a war that created victims and valiant heroes all across Europe and east into Asia, wreaking havoc even on the quiet beaches of the United States' own Hawaiian islands.

One of these Franciscans was a son of Italy. His country was gripped by Fascism under the dictatorship of Mussolini, over-run by the German army, and pummeled by Allied bombs, until it was slowly freed by the Allies' march north. Emilia Romagna, the northern region Fr. Faccenda called home, was the "communist capital" of Italy. It suffered the disastrous consequences – inevitable given the conditions of the war – nonetheless affecting thousands of persons who had been living simple, innocent, Catholic lives. Fr. Faccenda was one of these. He was ordained with the sound of Allied bombs literally thundering through the air, and volleys of German ground artillery rattling the long forgotten stillness of the air.

The other Franciscan you may know well. Fr. Maximilian's beloved Poland was nearly obliterated by the Nazi regime, terrified by the Red Army (despite its fragile – and often questioned – identity among the Allies) and ultimately rescued by Allied forces. Of course, St. Maximilian did not live to see this day of political liberation...

These men were not united merely by oppression at the hands of persons corrupted by false ideologies. Their communion did not exist only in a physical hunger, nor in the less tangible hunger for political freedom. These men shared in the thirst of Christ. They had an insatiable hunger for the salvation and happiness of souls. The same burning zeal and the same ardent love for the Immaculata drove them to heroic heights. Their bond is greater than physical proximity or familiarity. They are linked by their love for the Immaculate Mother of God.

St. Maximilian Kolbe, the martyr of Auschwitz, was declared by Pope John Paul II as "patron of our difficult times" (John Paul II, Assisi, Address at the Tomb of St. Francis, November 5, 1978). During his studies as a seminarian in Rome, when he was only twenty-three, Fr. Kolbe founded the Militia of the Immaculata (MI) with six other student friars. That was October 16, 1917. Ninety-five years later, this Marian and missionary Movement is officially recognized as a Public Association of the Faithful (Pontifical Council for the Laity, Decree of Erection, Vatican City, October 16, 1997). It is international, with membership reaching beyond 4 million. Its goal remains to "promote total consecration to the Virgin Mary for the purpose of spiritual renewal of individuals and society."

St. Maximilian also founded "Cities of the Immaculata," first in Poland (Niepokalanów) and later another in Japan (Mugenzai no Sono). These friaries were home to priests and brothers who used modern equipment to promote the MI via the mass media. At its height, Niepokalanów's publishing apostolate produced one million magazines monthly as well as 125,000 copies of a daily paper for the nearly one million members of the worldwide MI.

In 1941, Fr. Kolbe was imprisoned and sent to Auschwitz. After a prisoner had escaped in late July, ten men were chosen to die as punishment. St. Maximilian was not among the chosen, but he had been called to the highest imitation of Christ. He offered his life willingly to save that of a fellow prisoner. Ten days later, after leading his fellow prisoners in prayers and hymns, he was given a lethal injection of carbolic acid. Fittingly, it was August 14, 1941, the eve of the Assumption of the Blessed Virgin Mary. Fr. Kolbe was canonized by Pope John Paul II on October 10, 1982. He was the only saint in the Church's history to officially be recognized as a "martyr of charity."

Fr. Luigi Faccenda received and promoted the spiritual and apostolic legacy of Fr. Kolbe. He was born in a small village near Bologna, Italy, in 1920. When he was of age, he joined the Conventual Franciscans. In 1945, a year after his ordination, he was assigned to be director of the MI in Bologna. He had no program to follow or experience. In order to compensate for his lack of resources, he committed himself wholeheartedly to study the spirit of the MI. He researched the life and the charism of Fr. Kolbe – not an easy task only four years after the saint's martyrdom. Yet, Fr. Luigi Faccenda knew he had a mission.

Fr. Faccenda recalled that, as he was wondering about his specific place in God's plan, he had a spiritual encounter with Fr. Kolbe that changed his entire life. Looking at the example of his holy confrere, who freely gave up his life, offering to die on behalf of a father of two sons, Fr. Faccenda found God's will concerning his own life, his apostolate and his priesthood: "From that moment on I never stopped. I studied the mystery of Mary through the Church's teaching and I understood that we cannot be Christian without accepting and loving Mary, the Mother of God. I experienced her powerful mediation and I worked tirelessly so that schools, workplaces, families, hospitals, and human hearts could listen to Mary's voice and her maternal invitation through a solid Catholic doctrine" ("Omelie Sacerdotali," in Orientamenti di Vita Spirituale, X:131).

Fr. Faccenda concluded that the maternal mediation of Mary Immaculate, closely joined to her Son, the Redeemer of the world, and the action of the Holy Spirit, was the key to evangelization and the secret of holiness. He recalled: "I realized that in his Militia of the Immaculata Movement there was a secret which should have been known because in it many would have found hope." Just as Fr. Kolbe, in the face of hatred and atrocity, entered the darkness of the starvation cell, motivated by the purest love for God and his neighbors, so his life and testimony could be an inspiration for those who wanted to reach the fullness of Christian love.

Fr. Faccenda reflected on the spiritual bond uniting him to the life and message of Fr. Kolbe. When he received the honorary doctorate in theology (May 17, 1995), he stated: "I have come to understand, then, that St. Maximilian Kolbe's spiritual legacy is indeed limitless. Total consecration to the Immaculata with apostolic intents, which he lived and promoted, must be and is a true spirituality. Undoubtedly, Kolbe's is a very demanding legacy; for it requires imitation of him who made us his heirs. In fact, it is not a matter of possessing something of him (possible relics, an autograph, his biography, etc.), but of living his spirit. The legacy of the saints is above all what they did in response to God's will. To be their heirs means to allow God to work in us as He did in them—as He did in St. Maximilian Kolbe and in many of his followers."

Fr. Faccenda committed himself and the members of the Movement to evangelization. He strove to make known Mary's place in God's salvific plan by means of direct contact with different categories of people and by using the mass media. Fr. Faccenda's entire pastoral program was devoted to spreading Fr. Kolbe's ideal—consecration to the Immaculate Heart of Mary, culminating in the total giving of one's life.

In the 1950s, a group of young women asked to consecrate their lives to God in the spirit of St. Maximilian. Although at first Fr. Faccenda was hesitant, with the required permission and some valuable encouragement, he dedicated himself to establishing the Fr. Kolbe Missionaries of the Immaculata, a Secular Institute for consecrated women, founded in the Marian Year, 1954. This Institute received its definitive recognition as a Secular Institute of Pontifical Right in 1992.

Since its beginning, the Institute has aimed at achieving the perfect charity of its members and the fullness of their baptismal consecration, in order to be a Marian and missionary presence in the world. The incorporated members are consecrated lay women. They profess the evangelical counsels of poverty, chastity, and obedience and strive to live the total offering to the Immaculata following the teaching and the example of St. Maximilian Kolbe. They are called to be at the service of humanity in every environment and social class. They are to promote the knowledge and the veneration of the Virgin Mary, work at the formation of Christian conscience, and be active in the new evangelization. In the more than fifty years since its founding, the Institute has spread throughout Italy to Argentina, United States, Luxembourg, Bolivia, Poland, Brazil, and Mexico. Through its media apostolate it reaches yet further across South America and Europe, and through its Volunteers even into Africa.

It has increased its effectiveness with the help of associated members, the Fr. Kolbe Volunteers of the Immaculata, lay and clerical members who choose to share the spirituality and the mission of the Institute.

On February 11, 1997, the Fr. Kolbe Missionaries of the Immaculata for men began in Brazil, where an active national center of the MI exists, led by Fr. Sebastiano Quaglio. In a letter of February 20, 1997 announcing the beginning of this Institute, Fr. Faccenda wrote: "With my complete approval and fatherly blessing, six Brazilian young men have begun an experience of common life, led by the enlightened wisdom of Fr. Sebastiano. For a long time these young men have been molded in St. Maximilian's ideal. Conquered by his bold spirituality, they are seriously thinking of an institute with a missionary, Marian and Kolbean charism. A keen interest impels them: the desire to consecrate themselves totally for the cause of God's Kingdom, at the school and under the maternal guidance of Mary Immaculate, in order to be leaven of life for their fellow Brazilians and for all the people of the world, without distinguishing between nations or continents. ... The spirit which animates them is the same spirit that stirred St. Maximilian Kolbe and the first Missionary women."

Fr. Faccenda defines the Kolbean ideal as a total offering of oneself with apostolic intent. Strengthened by the lived example and teaching of the founder, both the male and female Institutes have always devoted themselves to evangelize in the name of Mary, using all appropriate means, especially the printed word and the media. The service of the Fr. Kolbe Missionaries includes teaching catechetical classes, parish missions, and family visitations. The Missionaries also animate centers of spirituality, retreats, Marian conferences and meetings, and collaborate in promoting the Militia of the Immaculata. As members of Secular Institutes, they may also carry out many kinds of professional jobs. Ultimately, each missionary is called to sanctify the world from within by seeking to instill Christian values in every environment they find themselves in. Mary is the example par excellence of living "in the world, for the world."

With his untiring activity, rooted in a profound life of prayer, Fr. Faccenda carried the golden thread of the cause of the Immaculata. He comprehended St. Maximilian's missionary spirit, his pastoral dynamism, and doctrinal insights, not only reproducing them, but also reinterpreting them with his striking originality. He has developed a program for living total consecration to the Immaculata and furnished a Marian spirituality with a deep ecclesial spirit. He has brought to fruition many of Fr. Kolbe's intuitions and insights.

But Fr. Faccenda is not alone. The multitudes of lay and consecrated men and women who have joined the MI and/or the Fr. Kolbe Missionaries and the Volunteers have been captivated by the same ideal. In many countries today they are contributing in the fields of evangelization, social communication, and human services. They are motivated by the conviction that Christ wishes to lead all to the Immaculata, so that her maternal kingdom might extend to every corner of the world and to every moment of history. It is in this kingdom, the Kingdom of the Sacred Heart of Jesus, where peace and supernatural joy will reign. Still more amazing, the Fr. Kolbe Missionaries know that this Kingdom is already here. It is their job to tell the world, one soul, one place, one moment at a time.

Bibliography

Faccenda, Luigi. "Father Kolbe, the Immaculata, and the Most Holy Trinity." *Conference given at the St. Bonaventure Pontifical Theological Faculty.* Rome, May 17, 1995.

—. *One More Gift.* West Covina, CA: Immaculata Press , 1990.

—. *Symbiosis: Contemplation and Action.* West Covina, CA: Immaculata Press, 1991.

Foster, Claude R. *Mary's Knight.* West Chester, PA: West Chester University Press, 2002.

Hoffman, Pio Maria. *Primacy of Christ.* Master's Thesis, St. John's Seminary, Dunwoodie: unpublished, 2007.

Kolbe, Maximilian. *Scritti di Massimiliano Kolbe.* Rome: ENMI, 1997.

Lisieux, Therese of. *Story of a Soul.* Kindle Edition. Public Domain Books, 2005.

Louvencourt, Jean-Francois. *St. Maximilian Kolbe: Friend and Doctor of Prayer.* CD-ROM. Libertyville, IL: Marytown Press, n.d.

"Militia of the Immaculate General Statutes." Rome: Centro Internazionale M.I., n.d.

Vaticana, Libreria Editrice. *Catechism of the Catholic Church.* 2nd. San Francisco, CA: Ignatius Press, 1994.

About the Author

Jillian E. Cooke was born and raised in California. She was consecrated to the Immaculata and enrolled in the Militia of the Immaculata at age twelve. At sixteen she began ministry within her local parish and the MI. In 2004 she graduated from Thomas Aquinas College with a BA in Liberal Arts. Shortly after graduation she went on a volunteer mission in Argentina with the Fr. Kolbe Missionaries of the Immaculata. It was there that she responded to the call to join this Secular Institute and begin her journey in the consecrated life. She entered in West Covina, California on June 5, 2005 and professed her first vows on February 13, 2010. In 2012 she earned her Master's Degree in Dogmatic Theology from Holy Apostles College and Seminary.

Jillian is currently active in youth and young adult ministry, serving the local Church and the Militia of the Immaculata in various ways. She is pursuing a Masters in Pastoral Theology at St. John's Seminary in Camarillo, California. Prayers for her continued spiritual and intellectual growth as she journeys toward permanent incorporation and perpetual vows as a Fr. Kolbe Missionary of the Immaculata are greatly appreciated!

If you have any questions or comments, please contact us or visit us on the web.

Father Kolbe
Missionaries
of the Immaculata

About the Publisher

Immaculata Press is the publishing house of the Father Kolbe Missionaries of the Immaculata in the United States.

Its mission is to empower Christians in the modern world to live their values. To this end, it offers books and printed materials that wish to answer the essential search for meaning, truth, and joy in life, with a special focus on the Blessed Virgin Mary and the testimony of St. Maximilian Kolbe.

Additional information and resources about the life and legacy of St. Maximilian Kolbe can be obtained by contacting:

Fr. Kolbe Missionaries of the Immaculata

531 East Merced Avenue
West Covina, CA 91790
626-917-0040
fkmissionaries@gmail.com
www.kolbemission.org

Marytown
National Shrine of St. Maximilian Kolbe

1600 West Park Avenue
Libertyville, IL 60048
847-367-7800
mail@marytown.com
www.marytown.com
www.consecration.com

MI International Center

Via S. Teodoro, 42
00186 Roma - Italy
011-39-06-679-3828
MIinternational@ofmconv.org
www.mi-international.org